Eyewitness
SOCCER

DON DU PÉTROLE HAHN POUR LES CHEVEUX

GRAND MATCH D'ASSOCIATION

1930s French hair oil
advertisement

1930s painting
of a goalkeeper

1900s soccer ball pumps

1900s
shin pads

1910s
shin pads

1930s
shin pads

Early
20th-century
soccer ball
stencils

Steven Pienaar
of South Africa

1966 World
Cup soccer ball

1905 match
holder

1998 World Cup soccer ball

Eyewitness
SOCCER

Written by
HUGH HORNBY

Photographed by
ANDY CRAWFORD

1912 soccer ball

in association with
THE NATIONAL FOOTBALL MUSEUM, UK

19th-century
jersey

1925 Australian
International shirt

1905 book
cover image

Early
20th-century
playing card

DK
LONDON, NEW YORK,
MELBOURNE, MUNICH, and DELHI

Project editor Louise Pritchard
Art editor Jill Plank
Assistant editor Annabel Blackledge
Assistant art editor Yolanda Belton
Managing art editor Sue Grabham
Senior managing art editor Julia Harris
Production Kate Oliver
Picture research Amanda Russell
DTP designers Andrew O'Brien and Georgia Bryer

THIS EDITION
Consultants Mark Bushell, David Goldblatt
Editors Kitty Blount, Andrea Mills, Sarah Phillips, Sue Nicholson,
Victoria Heywood-Dunne, Marianne Petrou
Art editors Andrew Nash, David Ball
Managing editors Julie Ferris, Camilla Hallinan
Managing art editors Owen Peyton Jones, Jane Thomas
Art director Martin Wilson
Associate publisher Andrew Macintyre,
Production editors Siu Yin Ho, Andy Hilliard, Melissa Latorre
Production controllers Jenny Jacoby, Pip Tinsley
DK picture library Rose Horridge, Myriam Megharbi, Emma Shepherd
Picture research Carolyn Clerkin, Will Jones, Rob Nunn

This Eyewitness ® Guide has been conceived by
Dorling Kindersley Limited and Editions Gallimard

First published in the United States in 2000, 2005, 2008
This revised edition published in the United States in 2010
by DK Publishing, 375 Hudson Street, New York, New York 10014

A catalog record for this book is
available from the Library of Congress.

ISBN: 978-0-7566-6294-3 (Hardcover)
ISBN: 978-0-7566-6295-0 (Library Binding)

Color reproduction by Colourscan,
Singapore, and MDP, UK
Printed and bound by
Toppan Printing Co., (Shenzen) Ltd., China

Discover more at
www.dk.com

THE REFEREE

1900s
plaster
figurine

1908
Newcastle
shirt

1900s silver
match
holder

1930s
silver
hatpin

1920s
silver flint
lighter

Shirts from 1890s catalog

Contents

Hungary pin Holland pin Italy pin Brazil pin

Early 20th-century child's rattle

1930s child's painted rattle

The global game

Soccer has its roots in ancient China, Europe, and the Americas. People kicked a ball to prepare for war, to honor their gods, or just to entertain themselves. For centuries, different versions of ball-kicking games existed. In Europe, they were tests of courage and strength and in China and other Eastern countries, the games were rituals of grace and skill. The rules of the modern game of soccer were not drawn up until 1863, but the qualities that we admire in it—speed, agility, bravery, and spirit—have been present in many cultures for more than 2,000 years.

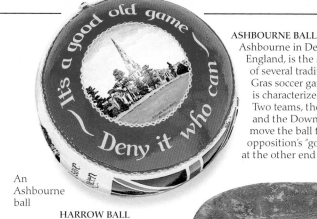

An Ashbourne ball

ASHBOURNE BALL
Ashbourne in Derbyshire, England, is the site of one of several traditional Mardi Gras soccer games. It is characterized by disorder. Two teams, the Upwards and the Downwards, try to move the ball through the opposition's "goal"—a gateway at the other end of town.

HARROW BALL
English private schools, including Harrow and Eton, played a crucial role in developing modern soccer in the early 1800s. Although each school played the game differently, they all produced detailed, written rules. These provided the basis for the first official rules.

The Harrow ball was flattened, top and bottom, to allow it to skim across muddy playing fields

SOCCER TRAINING
The Chinese were playing a type of soccer by the 3rd century BCE. A military book of that period refers to *tsu chu*, or "kicking a ball." The game may once have been part of a soldier's training and was later included in ceremonies on the emperor's birthday.

Chinese characters meaning "soccer"

A GENTLEMEN'S GAME
The game of calcio was played in Italian cities such as Venice and Florence in the 16th and 17th centuries. On certain festival days, two teams of gentlemen would attempt to force the ball through openings at either end of a city square. Although physical contact was a feature of calcio, the game also had a tactical element. Teams used formations and attempted to create space in which to advance.

Local people came out to watch the games

Handling the ball was part of the game

Players have to wear an elaborate costume of silk and gold brocade

Ball made from strips of leather

Men from many different backgrounds played soccer

STREET GAMES
This early 19th-century cartoon is subtitled "Dustmen, coalmen, gentlemen, and city clerks at murderous if democratic play." It shows the violent "every man for himself" spirit common to street games in Britain at that time. The damage done to property, particularly windows, and the disruption to the lives of other citizens caused many town councils to ban soccer—without much success.

ANCIENT RITUAL
The Japanese game of kemari probably developed in the 7th century from an ancient Chinese soccer game, after contact was made between the two countries. In contrast to the chaotic early soccer brawls of Europe, it involved many rituals and was played as part of a ceremony. The game is still played today and involves keeping the ball in the air inside a small court.

Kemari is a game of balance and skill

SOCCER WRITING
Soccer has been a popular literary subject for as long as the game has been played. The first-known book devoted to soccer is *Discourse on Calcio* by Giovanni da Bardi, published in 1580 in Florence, Italy. Soccer has inspired poetry, too. "A Match at Football" by Matthew Concanen was published in an anthology in the 18th century. The popularity of soccer increased rapidly in the early 20th century. *The School Across the Road* by Desmond Coke is one of many children's books published at around that time.

16th-century discourse on soccer

18th-century anthology

The children's book *The School Across the Road*

Color plates appear throughout the book

Image from a th-century watercolor on silk

7

History of soccer

THE GAME THAT HAS CAPTURED the imaginations of people all over the world was developed in England and Scotland in the 19th century. The former pupils of English private schools produced the first common set of rules for football, or soccer, and formed the Football Association (FA) in 1863. Things moved forward quickly. British administrators, merchants, and engineers took the game overseas and people from other countries began to play soccer. The first international games were followed by professional leagues and big competitions.

CELEBRITY PLAYER
The first players were amateurs. C. B. Fry, who played for the Corinthians in the late 1890s, was one of the first soccer celebrities. He was also a member of the England cricket team and held the world long-jump record.

Arnold Kirke Smith's cap

EXHIBITIONISM
Throughout the early years of the 20th century, British teams toured the world, introducing soccer to other countries by playing exhibition games. This shield was presented to the Islington Corinthians in Japan, in 1937.

Kinnaird once did a headstand after winning a Cup final

The English Three Lions motif was first used in 1872

Arnold Kirke Smith's England shirt

The shirt is made of closely woven wool

THE FIRST INTERNATIONAL
In November 1872, Scotland played England on a cricket field in Glasgow in the first-ever international match. About 2,000 spectators watched a 0–0 draw. This shirt and cap were worn by Arnold Kirke Smith from Oxford University, who was a member of the English team.

MODERN RULES
Lord Kinnaird was president of the Football Association from 1890–1923, and was one of the amateurs who shaped the rules and structure of the modern game. He played in nine of the first 12 FA Cup finals, winning five.

TALENTED TEAMS
The English Football League began in 1888. Its 12-team fixture program was inspired by US baseball. This 1893 painting by Thomas Hemy shows two successful clubs of the 1890s: Aston Villa which won the league five times and Sunderland, "the team of all talents," which won three times.

THE UNRULY GAME
The first French soccer league, set up in 1894, was dominated by teams of Scottish immigrants, such as the White Rovers and Standard AC. French satirists were quick to refer to the game's reputation for unruliness. This 1900s French magazine, *Le Monde Comique*, reflects this attitude toward the game.

Bystanders often got caught up in the boisterous action

Cover illustration entitled *"Les Plaisirs du Dimanche"* ("Sunday" Pleasures")

In reality, women's uniforms were less figure-hugging

A ball of exaggerated size

N° 720   NOUVELLE PÉRIODE   PRIX : 10 CENTIMES

LE MONDE COMIQUE
ILLUSTRÉ
JOURNAL HEBDOMADAIRE, 8, RUE SAINT-JOSEPH, 8, PARIS

Prix des Abonnements : Paris, un an, 6 fr. — Départements, un an, 8 fr. — Union postale, 10 fr. — Un Numéro par semaine

LES PLAISIRS DU DIMANCHE. — par DRANER

— Mille excuses, madame... je suis un peu myope.. je croyais lancer mon ballon

LADIES FIRST
Women's soccer started at the end of the 19th century. Teams such as the British Ladies Club attracted large crowds. During World War I, men's and women's teams played against each other for charity. The first women's World Cup was held in China in 1991 and was won by the USA.

FIFA pin

FORMING FIFA
By 1904, several countries, including France, Belgium, Denmark, the Netherlands, Spain, Sweden, and Switzerland had their own administrators. They formed the world governing body, FIFA (Fédération Internationale de Football Associations). By 1939, more than 50 countries had joined.

This 1900s plaster figurine is wearing shin pads that were typical of that time

Each stamp shows a different US player

US stamps produced for the 1994 World Cup

Ugandan batik

OUT OF AFRICA
Soccer spread through Africa from both ends of the continent. South Africa, with its European populations, was an obvious foothold and sent a touring party to South America in 1906. In 1923, Egypt became the first African team to join FIFA. In 2010, South Africa becomes the first African country to host the World Cup finals.

SOCCER
Youth soccer is the most widely played sport in the US, for both boys and girls. The 1994 World Cup Finals held in the US provided a big boost for Major League Soccer, which is bringing top-level professional games to a new audience.

Laws of the game

THE RULES OF A GAME should be brief and easy to understand. It is certain that soccer's success has been due partly to the simplicity of its Laws. Rules governing equipment, the field, foul play, and restarts have all survived the passage of time. Soccer has always been a free-flowing game. Stoppages can be avoided if the referee uses the advantage rule—allowing play to continue after a foul, providing that the right team still has the ball. The offside rule has always been a source of controversy in the game. The assistant referees must make split-second decisions about whether an attacker has strayed beyond the second-to-last defender at the moment the ball is played forward by one of his or her teammates. A player cannot be offside from a throw-in.

STAND BACK
This throw-in is illegal. The ball is held correctly in both hands but the feet, though they are both on the ground as they should be, are over the line.

There have been goal posts since the early days of soccer but, until the crossbar was introduced in 1875, tape was stretched between them 8 ft (2.5 m) from the ground

The penalty spot is 12 yd (11 m) from the goal line

Goal kicks must be taken from within the 6-yd (5.5-m) box

Players must not cross the halfway line until the ball is kicked off

PENALTY
Penalties were introduced in 1891 as a punishment for foul play, such as tripping, pushing, or handball within 12 yd (11 m) of the goal. A player shoots at goal from the penalty spot with only the goalkeeper to beat. If the ball rebounds from the post or bar the penalty taker cannot play it again before someone else has touched it.

FREE KICK
There are two types of free kick—direct and indirect. In an indirect free kick, awarded after an infringement of a Law, the ball must be touched by two players before a goal is scored. Direct free kicks are given after fouls and the taker may score immediately. Opposing players must be at least 10 yd (9 m) away from the ball at a free kick.

CORNER
A corner kick is taken when the defending team puts the ball out of play behind their own goal line. Corner kicks provide useful goal-scoring opportunities. The ball must be placed within the quadrant—a quarter circle with a radius of 1 yd (1 m) in the corner of the field. A goal can be scored directly from a corner kick.

FAKING FOULS
The amateur players of the 19th century believed that all fouls were accidental and would have been horrified by the "professional foul," an offense deliberately committed to preve an attack from developing. Unfortunately, the game today is f of deliberate fouls. Some players also fake being fouled to get their team a free kick.

When a penalty is taken, only the taker is allowed inside the "D"

CHARGE!
The 1958 English FA Cup final between Manchester United and Bolton Wanderers is remembered for the disputed goal scored by Bolton's center-forward, Nat Lofthouse. He charged the United goalkeeper, Harry Gregg, over the line as he caught the ball—a challenge that all referees today would consider a foul.

Players from the defending team must stay out of the 10-yd (9-m) circle before the kickoff

Players cannot be offside in their own half of the field

The 6-yd (5.5-m) box was semicircular until 1902. The penalty box was introduced in the same year

...ssistant ...ferees patrol ...pposite sides of the ...eld and cover one ...lf each, their main ...sponsibilities being to signal ...row-ins and flag for offside

...AW AND ORDER
...here are 17 main soccer Laws. The field ...f play must be rectangular and, for a full-size ...eld, from 110 to 120 yd (100.5 to 110 m) long and ...om 70 to 80 yd (64 to 73 m) wide. There should be ...1 players per side. Substitution rules have changed over ...e years and teams may now substitute any three from five ...ayers, including the goalie, during stoppages in the match. The ...uration of play is 90 minutes, in two halves of 45 minutes each.

PERMANENT MARKERS
In the mid-19th century, before it was stipulated that permanent lines should be marked on the field, flags were used as a guide to whether the ball was out of play. Today, a corner flag has to be at least 5 ft (1.5 m) high so players do not risk being impaled.

Goal nets, patented by Brodies of Liverpool, England, in 1891, were first officially used in 1892 and were welcomed as a means of settling disputes over whether a ball had actually entered the goal

The referee

Early 20th-century playing card caricature of a referee

THE REFEREE

Early amateur players put a high value on fair play but saw the need for officials on the soccer field. To begin with, each team provided an umpire from its own club, who did not interfere much with the passage of play. At this stage, players had to raise an arm and appeal for a decision if they felt that they had been fouled, otherwise play continued. The rise of professional soccer in the 1880s made it harder for umpires to be neutral. A referee was introduced to settle disputes. In 1891, the referee was moved onto the field of play and the umpires became linesmen, a system that has continued ever since. Linesmen and women are now called assistant referees.

YOUR NUMBER'S UP
One duty of the assistant referee is to control the entrance of substitutes onto the field and check their studs. At top levels of the game, a fourth official uses an illuminated board to indicate the shirt number of the substitute and the player being replaced and inform everyone how much injury time will be played at the end of each half.

CLASSIC BLACK
This is the classic referee's uniform, all-black with white cuffs and collar. Dating from the 1970s, this uniform is similar to those worn after the phasing out of the blazer in the 1940s to the introduction of other colors in the 1990s. The bulky jackets of the early 1900s were replaced by a less constricting shirt to encourage the officials to keep up with play on the field.

White trim sets off the all-black uniform

Notebook to record bookings, goals, sendings off, and substitutions

The yellow card is shown for bookable offenses

Serious foul play results in a red card and a sending off

1940s Acme whistle

Both sides of a FIFA Fair Play coin

Badge refers to the referee's local association

Referees must be neatly dressed, with shirt tucked in at all times

Referees may carry a handkerchief in case players get dirt in their eyes

TOOLS OF THE TRADE
Certain items are vital to the referee's job. Red and yellow cards may seem like a long-established part of soccer but they were introduced only in the 1970s. It is believed the whistle was first used in 1878 and it was soon recognized as the best way of controlling play. Barrel-shaped whistles used to predominate but other shapes are now common. The referee carries a notebook and pencil to record details of the game and a special coin that is tossed to decide which team kicks off and in which direction.

U'RE BOOKED

okings used to be given only
:e or twice per match and
dings off were extremely rare,
: FIFA now insists that referees
much stricter. As a result, teams
ularly have to play with 10 team
mbers, or even fewer.

A red card is shown when a player has committed two bookable offenses

A whistle is blown to indicate the start or restart of play, or to stop play due to a foul or injury

JPNKULOVSKI 18

Referees have to be in shape to keep up with play on the field

Former USSR

Australia

New Zealand

Bangladesh

Iceland

Portugal

USA

Colombia

Italy

WORLD-CLASS REFEREES

These pins are produced by Referees' Associations around the world. Despite all the abuse they receive, referees are motivated by the prospect of officiating at top-class games. World Cup matches are controlled by officials from all countries affiliated to FIFA, not just those that qualify as competitors.

LINESMAN
FIFA
92

LINESWOMAN
FIFA
95

Official FIFA badges for sewing on the officials' shirts

Men and women officiate at top-level soccer matches

TOUCHLINE HELPERS

The first linesmen waved a handkerchief to alert the referee. Assistant referees today use a flag. They wave the flag when a player is offside, when the ball is out of play, and when they have seen an infringement on the field.

The first referees wore knickers

Blazer with pockets for a stopwatch and notebook

HOW TO BE A REFEREE

This illustration from the cover of a 1906 book entitled *How to be a Referee* shows the typical referee's clothing of that period. After taking an exam, referees usually start out at amateur level. They are assessed regularly to ensure that standards remain high. Today's top referees are professional. They earn good salaries for officiating top games.

The field

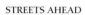
This Samuel Brandão painting shows soccer being played on a dirt field in Rio de Janeiro, Brazil

AT THE START OF A SEASON, players can look forward to playing their first game on a smooth green field. If a field is not looked after, it soon becomes muddy and uneven, especially if cold, wet weather sets in. Groundskeepers try to keep the fields in good condition with the help of new species of grass and good drainage. In many northern European countries, soccer takes a midwinter break during the worst conditions. Wealthy clubs may lay a completely new field between games, but millions of amateur players have to make do with whatever muddy or frozen land is available.

STREETS AHEAD
In the days before traffic became too heavy, street soccer was a popular pastime. Children learned close ball control and dribbling skills in confined spaces. They often used heaps of clothes or gateways as goalposts.

Groundskeepers preparing for a game during the 1953 English season

Jean-Pierre Papin playing for AC Milan, Italy, on a snow-covered field

PLAYING IN SNOW
In snowy weather, the field markings and the white soccer ball are hard to see and the ground is slippery. If the markings can be swept clear and the field is soft enough to take a stud, play can usually carry on, using a more visible orange ball.

HOT STUFF
In countries where the weather is cold during the soccer season, many methods have been tried to prevent fields from freezing. Undersoil heating was first installed in England at Everton in 1958. Before undersoil heating became common, groundskeepers put straw down as insulation and lit fires in braziers to lift the air temperature. Today, large covers are sometimes used to protect fields.

SLOPES AND SHADE

Modern fields such as Preston (*above*) are usually laid with a camber, which means that they slope slightly down from the center circle to the touchlines. This helps to drain water away. When large stands are built, less air and light reach the grass, stunting its growth. This has been a problem at some stadiums, such as the San Siro in Milan, Italy.

Grass is kept long to encourage deep rooting

Layer of top soil nourishes the grass

Heating pipes laid in grids

Layers of sand and gravel allow water to filter away

PAMPERING THE FIELD

Modern field maintenance is a full-time job. In the summer, the grass must be mowed, watered, and fed regularly. During the close season, work is done to repair holes and worn patches in the turf. New types of grass have been developed that grow better in the shade of tall stands. This is vital in helping the groundskeepers to keep the field in good condition.

The surface is made to mimic grass

Fibers are woven together to form a carpet

Artificial grass viewed from the side, top, and underneath

The base of the field is composed of large pieces of stone

Drainage pipes carry away water

Model of a section through a field

BETTER THAN THE REAL THING?

Artificial fields are made from synthetic turf laid on a shock-absorbent pad. They are more hard-wearing than grass fields and are unaffected by torrential rain or freezing cold. Clubs with an artificial field can rent out their stadium for a range of events, such as concerts, and their home games need never be postponed because of bad weather. Many players do not like the surface because they feel that it increases the risk of injury.

SATURATION POINT

Rainwater is the greatest threat to field condition. Good built-in drainage is therefore an important part of field construction. Pipes and materials chosen for their good draining qualities are laid under the grass. A large amount of sand is mixed into the top soil to make it less absorbent and less prone to becoming waterlogged. Even a well-cared-for field may become saturated. Groundskeepers sometimes have to resort to using garden forks to remove standing water.

Soccer skills

Early 20th-century button showing a man heading the ball

Eᴀᴄʜ ᴘᴏsɪᴛɪᴏɴ ᴏɴ ᴛʜᴇ ғɪᴇʟᴅ is associated with a specific range of tasks. Defenders must be able to tackle the opposition and claim the ball, midfielders need to pass the ball accurately to their teammates, and strikers have to shoot and score goals. Although most players specialize in a certain position, professional players are expected to master a range of skills and work on any weaknesses. As part of their daily training routine, they practice hard to perfect their skills so that their technique does not let them down in a game.

CONTROL FREAK
The best players, like England's Wayne Rooney, can always bring the ball under control. To deal with high passes, players need to keep their eyes on the ball and use their chest, stomach, head or, like Rooney here, their thighs to stun the ball.

Players call out to each other to indicate their intentions on the ball

TACKLE TALK
Players try to take the ball from another player by tackling. Italy's Fabio Cannavaro, the only defender to win the FIFA Player of the Year award, is a great tackler. He shows the perfect timing that is essential to avoid committing a foul. Referees punish players if they make a physical challenge from behind or if they make contact with a player instead of the ball.

PASS MARK
Moving the ball quickly around the field, from one player to another, is the most effective means of stretching a defense. Accurate passing remains the hallmark of all successful teams. Barcelona's star passer of the ball is Xavi. He has the vision to pass the ball into space for his strikers even when he is tightly marked.

Constant movement into space is essential

The player must time his leap to meet the ball firmly

If the defender is unable to reach the ball, he must still challenge the striker

All parts of the foot are used to manipulate the ball in the desired direction

The ability to pass with both feet gives the player more options

HEADS UP!
There are two distinct kinds of heading, defensive and attacking. Defenders try to gain distance when they clear a high ball out of the goal area. Attackers need accuracy and power to score goals with a header. Chelsea striker Didier Drogba uses his height to beat the opposition and head the ball into the net.

Keeping the head still improves accuracy

Crosses, or passes in from the wings, result in more goals than any other angle of attack. Players who can put the ball over with pace and accuracy are extremely valuable to a team. Portugal and Real Madrid winger Cristiano Ronaldo arguably takes the world's greatest free kicks. He is able to put great power behind the ball while also applying curve or dip. He plants his left foot firmly alongside the ball and uses his arms to maintain balance before driving his right foot through the ball. The way his foot strikes the ball dictates the dip or curl required.

The player can pretend to go in one direction before going in the other

Extending the arms assists with balance

DOWNTOWN DRIBBLER
When a player runs with the ball at his feet, it is called dribbling. Brazilian star Ronaldinho, who learned his soccer on the streets of Porto Alegre, is proof that dribbling can cause problems for the opposition. Good balance and concentration help a dribbler to change direction quickly and ride tackles.

Keeping body weight over the ball makes it easier to cross with power

The foot turns in as it passes through the ball to make it swerve

The bicycle kick is even harder if the ball is moving across the player

Leaning back helps to ensure that the ball will rise toward the top of the net

GOING FOR THE GOAL
When shooting, forwards need the accuracy to find the corner of the net as well as the power to blast the ball through the defense. Samuel Eto'o of Cameroon beats goalkeepers regularly with his powerful right foot.

The left leg is firmly planted to allow the body to make the best shape for the cross

BICYCLE KICK
The bicycle kick was first demonstrated in the 1930s by Brazilian forward Leonidas. It is one of the most difficult skills to pull off. With their backs to the goal, strikers throw their legs up in the air and kick the ball while falling backward. This tactic sometimes catches the goalkeeper by surprise. This model of Italian striker Roberto Baggio shows the ideal body position.

A higher jump allows the player to keep the ball down below the crossbar

A 1900s match holder showing a goalkeeper punching clear

The goalkeeper

AS THE LAST LINE of defense, a goalkeeper knows that a single mistake can cost the team victory. Goalkeeping can be a lonely job. It entails having different skills from the rest of the team and you can be unoccupied for several minutes at a time. The recent change to the back-pass law, forcing the goalkeeper to kick clear rather than pick up the ball, has made the job even harder. The necessity of having both a physical presence and great agility means that goalkeepers have to train as hard as any other player, but the reward for this diligence can be a much longer career than that of their teammates.

Clothes

Until 1909, goalkeepers were distinguishable only by their cap, making it difficult for the referee to judge who, in a goalmouth scramble, was handling the ball. From 1909 to the early 1990s, they wore a shirt of a single plain color that was different from the shirts worn by the rest of their team. A rule was made forbidding short sleeves, but it has now been relaxed.

GOOD SAVE
This 1950 comic cover shows the save that is considered to be the easiest to make—from a shot straight to the midriff. It also hints at the spectacular action in which goalkeepers are regularly involved, such as when they have to fly through the air to tip the ball away. Modern strikers are likely to make the ball swerve suddenly, so it is all the more important for goalies to keep their bodies in line with the ball.

CATCH IT
Punching the ball away from the danger area has always been popular among European and South American goalkeepers. The goalkeeper depicted on this 1900 book cover is trying to punch the ball but he probably should be trying to catch it because he is not being closely challenged. In the modern game, referees rarely allow goalkeepers to be charged when they are attempting to catch the ball.

The ball should be punched out toward the wing

KEEPERS' COLORS
Patterns in soccer shirts have traditionally been limited to stripes and hoops, but since the rules on goalkeepers' clothes were relaxed, every combination of colors seems to have been tried. Not all of them have been easy on the eye, although fluorescent designs are easy for defenders to see.

Flexible plastic ribs reinforce each finger

Modern gloves help to prevent injuries such as broken fingers

The shamrock, symbol of Ireland

EIRE SHIRT
This shirt was worn by Alan Kelly for the Republic of Ireland. He made 47 appearances, the first against West Germany in 1957 and the last against Norway in 1973. Yellow shirts were once a common sight in international games. Green was not an option for the Irish goalkeeper, because the uniform, or strip, of the Irish team is green.

GOALIE'S GLOVES
Until the 1970s, gloves were worn only when it was wet, and they were made of thin cotton. Modern goalkeepers wear gloves in all conditions. Various coatings and pads are used to increase the gloves' grip, which is the key to handling the ball.

Goalkeepers may still wear a cap if the sun is in their eyes

Arms are outstretched, ready to block a shot

NARROWING THE ANGLE
This image from the 1930s shows a goalkeeper alert to danger. When an attacker approaches the goal with the ball, goalkeepers should leave their line and move toward the ball to reduce the target area for the attacker. This "narrowing of the angle" is an important part of keepers' roles. They often make marks, in line with the posts, to help them keep their bearings when leaving the line.

LOUD AND CLEAR
Italy's and Juventus's exceptional goalkeeper Gianluigi Buffon controls his penalty area by shouting instructions to his team-mates. This loud communication ensures the defenders line up in the best way to create a wall for a free kick or organize themselves effectively in the penalty area for a corner kick.

Goalkeepers shout at their teammates to get the best protection during set pieces

Goalkeepers have to point when organizing the defensive wall for a free kick

THROWING OUT
This painted button from the 1900s shows one of the goalkeeper's jobs. A quick throw out, particularly after catching a corner, can be an effective way of launching an attack. Some goalkeepers are renowned for the length of their throw.

GOAL KICK
When the ball is put out behind the goal line by an attacker, the opposing team is awarded a goal kick. The goalkeeper takes the kick from inside the 6-yard (5.5-m) box. Early leather balls absorbed water and increased in weight, so a goal kick rarely reached the opposition's half.

Tactics

P ART OF SOCCER'S appeal is its tactical element. Coaches and managers try to outwit the opposition by keeping their tactics secret until the game. Since soccer first began, teams have lined up in different formations trying to play in a way that will take the other team by surprise and result in a goal. Early players had the physical attributes and skills needed for a particular position on the field. Today, the pace of the game demands that players be adaptable enough to play in almost any position, in the manner of the Dutch "total soccer" teams of the 1970s.

Old Arabic print of team formations

Center-half defended and attacke

2-3-5 formation (left)

Center-half only defended

W-M formation (right)

France won the 1998 World Cup with a back four

Wingers have been replaced by midfielders who can also defend

4-4-2 formation (right)

One forward often plays "in the hole" behind the other

Wing-backs are responsible for providing attacking width

Sweeper must be creative and pass accurately

Sweeper system (left)

IN GOOD FORM (ABOVE)
The 2-3-5 formation dominated tactics until the 1930s. Each player had a very specific place and role on the field. Herbert Chapman of Arsenal, England, was the first manager to make a radical change, positioning the center-half and inside-forwards deeper to create the W-M formation.

GAME PLAN (ABOVE)
Managers use a board like this in the dressing room. They use it to show players how to counteract the opposition and where they should be at certain points in the game. This is particularly important when defending corners and free kicks.

CLEAN SWEEP
Modern formations are very varied, but the 4-4-2 is one of the most popular. The four defenders are not expected to push forward and the four midfielders sometimes switch to a diamond shape. The sweeper system, perfected by the Italians in the 1960s, frees one player from marking duties to act as cover.

PACKED DEFENSE
Denial of space to the opposition forwards is vital and certain players may be singled out for man-to-man marking. It is often said that the best teams are built from the back, with a strong defense providing a springboard for attack. Here, England defenders are surrounding a striker.

The defenders are physically blocking in the attacker

The attacker is trapped

The forward cannot go "one on one" with the goalkeeper

OFFSIDE ORIGINS
The first offside law, in 1866, stated that three defenders, including the goalkeeper, had to be between the attacker and the goal when the ball was being played forward by a teammate. By 1920, fewer and fewer goals were being scored because, even if attackers were onside at the vital point, they still had to beat the last outfield defender.

Player is onside

OFFSIDE UPDATED
In 1925, FIFA decided to amend the offside law so that only two players had to be between the attacker and the goal. Immediately, far more goals were scored. The offside rule is basically unchanged today. Here, the midfielder is about to pass the ball to the forward. This player is still onside and, once in possession of the ball, will have only the goalkeeper to beat.

Player is offside

OFFSIDE TRAP
Teams without a sweeper, like Norway under Egil Olsen, are still able to use an offside trap. As the midfielder prepares to pass the ball forward, the defenders suddenly advance up the field in a line, leaving the forward offside when the ball is played. William McCracken of Newcastle, England, was famous for first perfecting this tactic, in the years before World War I.

NO SUBSTITUTE
Substitutions were first allowed by FIFA in 1923, but only if a player was injured. Injuries were faked so often to let coaches make tactical changes that it was gradually accepted that one player could be freely replaced. Now the number of substitutes allowed per team has increased to five for some games.

BE PREPARED
Javier Zanetti's goal for Argentina against England at France '98 was an example of how a well-rehearsed routine can work brilliantly. Lots of goals are scored from set-pieces—movements that a team practices before a game. Coaches spend a great deal of time going through these with the team in training.

Injury time

Mr, Black, the player from a Happy Families card game

A PROFESSIONAL PLAYER'S job involves far more than playing games and enjoying the limelight. Training, fitness, and recovery from injuries are day-to-day concerns for the modern player. Advances in medicine mean that injuries that a few years ago would have led to inevitable retirement can now be successfully treated. The pace of the modern game is unrelenting and loss of fitness is likely to stop a player from staying at the top level. Physical therapy, nutrition, and even psychology are all parts of the conditioning program of big clubs today.

FIGHTING FIT
Medicine balls like this were used in soccer training for many decades. They are extremely heavy, so throwing them improves stamina and also builds muscle bulk. Sophisticated gym equipment, training programs, and resistance machines are now commonly used. Strength and fitness are essential to success in the modern game because top players have to play as many as 70 games per season. The greatest players are superb athletes as much as they are skilled soccer players.

VITAL EDGE
Vittorio Pozzo, one of the first great managers, led Italy to victory in the World Cup in 1934 and 1938. He realized the importance of physical fitness and made his team train hard to give them a vital edge over their opponents. This paid off in extra time in the 1934 final, when Italy eventually scored the winning goal.

WARM UP AND COOL DOWN
A correct game-day routine can help to prolong a player's soccer career. Modern players are aware of the importance of warming up thoroughly before a game. The risk of muscle tears and strains is significantly reduced if the muscles are warm and loose. Recovery after games is also important. Many teams "warm down" after a game to relax their muscles before resting them.

The stretcher is carried by two wooden poles

A pillow is built into the stretcher

A piece of canvas supports the injured player

GETTING CARRIED AWAY
This stretcher was used in the 1920s. In those days, if the stretcher was brought out on the field, the crowd knew that a player was seriously injured. Today, players are given a few moments to get up before they are carried off to prevent time wasting and a delay to the game. They often run on again shortly afterward. In the US, motorized carts have taken the place of traditional stretchers.

AS IF BY MAGIC
The "magic" sponge has a special place in soccer folklore. Spectators have often wondered how a rubdown with a sponge and cold water could result in a player's swift recovery from an injury. Today, the team physical therapist, rather than the trainer, treats players for injury problems on the field and off it. Physical therapists are qualified to give sophisticated treatment to injured players.

The sponge is still used in amateur games

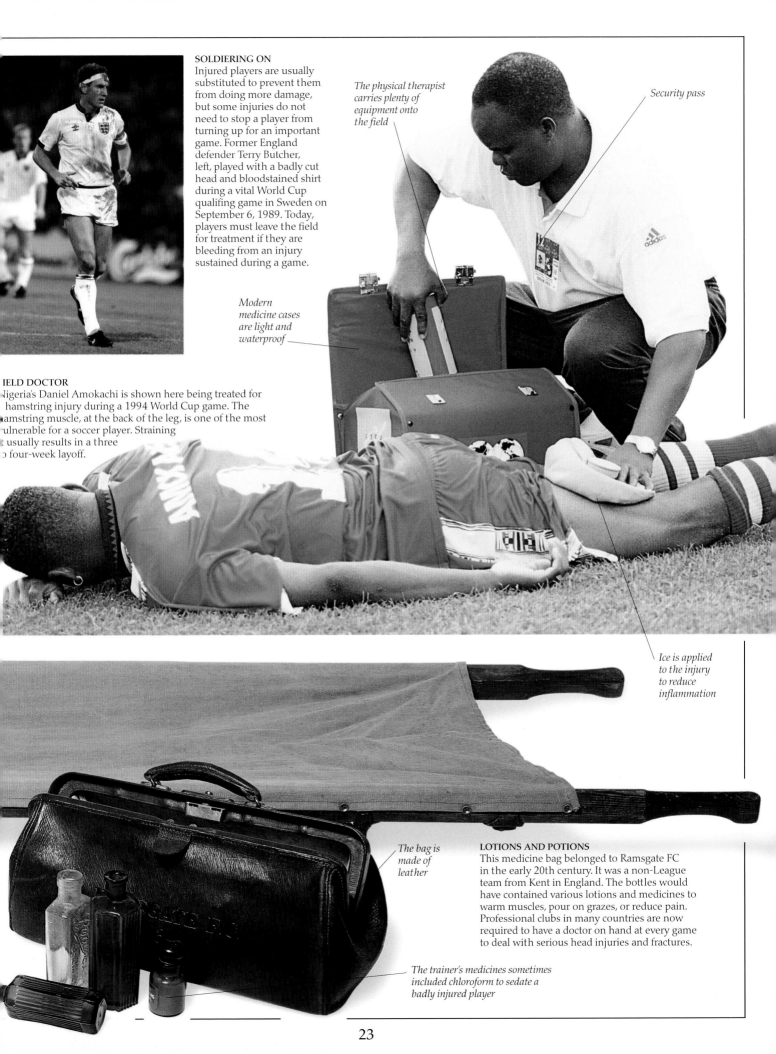

SOLDIERING ON
Injured players are usually substituted to prevent them from doing more damage, but some injuries do not need to stop a player from turning up for an important game. Former England defender Terry Butcher, left, played with a badly cut head and bloodstained shirt during a vital World Cup qualifing game in Sweden on September 6, 1989. Today, players must leave the field for treatment if they are bleeding from an injury sustained during a game.

The physical therapist carries plenty of equipment onto the field

Security pass

Modern medicine cases are light and waterproof

IELD DOCTOR
Nigeria's Daniel Amokachi is shown here being treated for hamstring injury during a 1994 World Cup game. The amstring muscle, at the back of the leg, is one of the most ulnerable for a soccer player. Straining t usually results in a three o four-week layoff.

Ice is applied to the injury to reduce inflammation

The bag is made of leather

LOTIONS AND POTIONS
This medicine bag belonged to Ramsgate FC in the early 20th century. It was a non-League team from Kent in England. The bottles would have contained various lotions and medicines to warm muscles, pour on grazes, or reduce pain. Professional clubs in many countries are now required to have a doctor on hand at every game to deal with serious head injuries and fractures.

The trainer's medicines sometimes included chloroform to sedate a badly injured player

Soccer balls

An 1890s brass traveling inkwell in the shape of a soccer ball

MUCH OF THE APPEAL of soccer lies in the fact that it can be played without any special equipment. Children everywhere know that a tin can, some bound-up rags, or a ball from a different sport entirely, can be satisfyingly kicked around. This ingenuity was first displayed hundreds of years ago, when people discovered that an animal's bladder could be inflated and knotted to provide a light, bouncy ball. A bladder alone did not last very long when kicked, so people began to protect the bladders in a shell made of animal skin cured to turn it into leather. This design worked so well that it is still used today but with modern, synthetic materials rather than animal products.

HEAVY GOING
Balls of the 1870s were often formed by stitching together eight segments of leather, the ends of which were secured by a central disk. The leather was unprotected and could absorb water on wet days, so that the ball increased in weight. Heading the ball could be dangerous, even fatal, and so this technique was not often used in those days. The dribbling game was the popular style and the heavy ball was suitable for this style of play.

Manufacturers' names were first stenciled on balls in about 1900

Sections of leather sewn together

The lace for tightening the case stands proud

Interlocking panels of leather

Tool for lacing the ball tightly

MADE TO MEASURE
This ball was used in March 1912, in the international match between Wales and England at Wrexham, Wales. England won the game 2–0. Made from a pig's bladder wrapped in cowhide, it is typical of the type of ball used for most of the 20th century. The outside shell was laced up. The size and weight of soccer balls were standardized for the first FA Challenge Cup competition in 1872, but the balls still absorbed water and were prone to losing their shape.

Copper stencil

The colors are based on the French flag

Brand name marked on the ball with a stencil

WORLD CUP COLORS
The first World Cup balls to have a color other than black were used in the Finals in France in 1998. They had a shiny, synthetic coating to make them waterproof and incorporated a layer of foam between the latex bladder and polyester skin. This let players pass and shoot quickly and also put spin and swerve on the ball. Like 75 percent of the world's soccer balls, they were made in the Sialkot region of Pakistan.

HEADING FOR TROUBLE
Balls like this were used in the 1966 World Cup Finals, at which time ball design had hardly changed in 50 years. The leather case was backed with a lining, a development of the 1940s that improved durability. The outside was painted with a pigment that helped to repel some water from a rain-soaked field. Manufacturers had still not found a reliable alternative to lacing up the ball so players risked injury when they headed the ball.

he handle is pushed
to the cylinder to
pump up the bladder

he piston
pels air
om the pump

ae
esthill
ass
mp

ae
kometer
easures
r pressure

mp is used when
anding upright

Pressure valve

Pump from
1893
equipment
catalog

Tube to
attach the
pump to the
ball's valve

PATCHING THINGS UP
This 1970s repair kit would have
been used with a vinyl ball. The
metal rod was heated and then
inserted into the puncture to
create a hole of the right
size, onto which a patch
could be glued.

Pump is
inserted
straight into
the ball

Patch with
"nipple"
to fit
the hole

Glue

Spare
valve

Metal
rod

BALL BOYS
This 17th-century German engraving shows that
inflated animal bladders have been used in ball
games for a long time. The two men depicted are servants preparing a
spare ball for their masters, who would have been playing pallone, a
soccer-type game that was played in 17th-century northern Europe.

1630 engraving
created by
Matthaus Merian
the Older

ULL OF AIR
ver time, air escaped from a ball's
adder and a pump was used to reinflate
Sometimes, the air pressure in a bladder
as increased to improve the bounce of
e ball. If a bladder was pumped up too
gh it was likely to burst, so some pumps
me with their own pressure gauge.
hese pumps date from the 1890s.

Calcio balls are made
of leather that is
stitched together
and then painted

The use of two colors
makes the Orkney ball
flash in the air

Alternative balls

everal different football games
re played around the world today.
hey each use a ball particular to
hat game. Some of these games
ave existed for centuries. The balls
ay have features connected
o a ceremonial aspect of
he game, and involve
ecoration and color, or
hey may be designed
o withstand harsh
reatment. In some
nodern games the
all has evolved
long with the game.

SHAPING UP
The game of American football
was originally based on
kicking a ball. As
throwing became a
central feature, the
present shape of
the ball evolved.
The small ball can
be gripped firmly,
making it easier for
the quarterback to
make long, accurate passes.

Cooper
OFFICIAL
191

BUILT TO LAST
In the Scottish Orkney
Isles, a type of football,
or soccer, game is played
through the streets every
New Year. The ball is
much heavier than a
normal soccer ball and is
stuffed tightly with pieces
of cork. This helps it to
last for several hours of
play and also makes it
float on water—a useful
feature because a team can
score a goal by throwing
the ball into the sea.

MADE TO MATCH
Calcio, first played in Italy
in the 16th century, was
reintroduced to Florence
in 1930. The game is played
by teams of 27 a side, all
wearing medieval clothes
and armor. Balls of various
colors are used, including
green, white, and red
to match the costumes.
Calcio balls are smaller
than regular soccer balls,
making it easier for the
players to pick them up
and throw them.

Soccer cleats

A 1950s painting of soccer boots called *Christopher's Boots*, by Doris Brand

O� ᴀʟʟ sᴏᴄᴄᴇʀ equipment, cleats, or boots, as they are sometimes known, have changed the most over the last 100 years. Always the most expensive item of gear, they remain an unaffordable luxury to many players around the world, who have to play in bare feet. The fast, agile sport we see today would simply not be possible if players had to wear the heavy, cumbersome shoes worn until the 1930s. Professionals then dreaded having to "break in" hard, new boots, which involved a great deal of pain. They preferred to patch up an old pair again and again until it fell apart. In the first World Cup tournaments in the 1930s, the South American teams wore lighter, low-cut boots, to the astonishment of the Europeans. These began the trend toward the modern, high-tech cleat.

MULTIPURPOSE BOOTS
In the late 1800s, very few people playing soccer would have had special footwear. These girls' boots could also have been worn to school or in the house. The smooth soles, pronounced heel, and extremely high cut would have seriously constricted movement, but the ankle would have been well protected.

19th-century girls' boots

1920s child's boots

A "kick around" is a popular pastime with children

MADE FOR THE JOB
By the 1920s, soccer boots like the "Manfield Hotspur" were being mass-produced for players of all ages. Children's boots were designed just like adults', with reinforced toe caps and heels, some ankle protection, and leather studs. Social conditions at the time, though, meant that most working-class families could not afford such equipment and, if they could, they would have handed down boots from one child to another.

Extra foot support

Cotton laces

STUDLESS BOOTS
A 19th-century gentleman player wore studless boots, which would not have allowed for sharp turns or long passing. However, they were practical enough for the type of dribbling game favored by the great English amateur teams like the Corinthians. This style of play was dictated by the confined spaces used for soccer practice at many British private schools. Boots like these would have doubled in weight when wet.

BOOTS IN THE BATH
In 1910 these boots were marketed as "Cup Final Specials," an early example of a soccer product being tied to a famous match. The wickerwork pattern on the toes was one of several designs that were thought to help a player control the ball—a major part of modern shoe design, too. It was common for a player to wear a new pair of shoes in the bathtub for a few hours to soften the leather.

LOTS OF LACES
Paton's bootlaces, in various colors, were widely used from the 1930s onward. There was a constant demand for replacements because repeated soaking during games, followed by drying out, caused the early cotton laces to perish and eventually snap.

SPONSORSHIP DEALS
Over the last 50 years, star players, such as Barcelona's Thierry Henry, have received huge sums of money to wear popular brands of soccer cleats. Corporate companies sponsor players to raise the profile and boost the sales of their brand of cleats. Many players donate their used cleats to charity or give them to club museums if they were worn during significant games.

White laces were common in the 1930s

England's Tom Finney promoted these boots

THE DESIGNER AGE
A vast amount of money is spent on the research and development of modern cleats. Top-quality leather uppers, usually made from kangaroo hides, and light, synthetic soles combine to make cleats that last. They are comfortable and allow the best players to put amazing amounts of spin on the ball. LA Galaxy's star David Beckham wears a new pair of cleats for every game, and this pair was specially designed to include the names of his sons.

⁞E MODERN LOOK
⁞ classic black-with-white-trim ⁞ign, which is still used today, ⁞ame popular in the 1950s. The ⁞ical strap on the instep remains ⁞ earlier designs. The cleats were ⁞oming flexible enough to be worn ⁞hout much breaking-in. There ⁞ less protection around the ankle, ⁞ch allowed players more freedom ⁞ movement but led to an increase ⁞ njuries. It was at this time that ⁞emakers began to use the name of ⁞ous players to sell their products.

⁞tuds and stuff
⁞e number of studs, or cleats, on the sole, ⁞d the way in which they are positioned, ⁞ries greatly. Longer studs are needed if ⁞ field is wet and muddy, shorter ones ⁞ worn if the field is hard. The potential ⁞y have to cause injury has always ⁞en a concern to the game's governing ⁞dies—in the 1930s, the wearing of ⁞gal shoes was a sending-off offense. ⁞ce 1900, one of the jobs of the referee ⁞ an assistant has been to check the cleats ⁞every player entering the field of play. ⁞ybody wearing cleats with sharp edges ⁞ protruding nails is not allowed to play.

Wooden hammer

Nails fixed to cleats

Separate nails

Cleats are screwed into the sole

Key for tightening the cleats

THE FIRST CLEATS
Early soccer boots were made entirely of leather. The cleats had to be hammered into the soles.

HARMFUL HAMMERS
Rubber cleats came next. They also needed to be nailed to the sole and it was not long before the boots were damaged.

ALL CHANGE!
Modern screw-in cleats are made of plastic or metal. Players can change their cleats at half-time, to adjust to changes in conditions.

Soccer outfits

Shirts, shorts, and socks were described as the basis of a soccer player's outfit in the first Laws of 1863, and they remain so today. The materials used for a player's outfit have changed since then. Players in South America and Mediterranean countries needed clothing suitable for warm climates, so wool gave way to cotton and then artificial fibers. Cool fabrics that "breathe" are now the norm worldwide. Teams wear matching outfits, or strips, on the field of play. The colors are the club colors, with which all the fans can identify. Most clubs and international sides have a home and an away strip in case two teams wear the same colors.

In the 19th century, both soccer and rugby players wore knee-length knickerbockers with no leg protection

DUTCH ORANGE
The Holland uniform is unusual in being orange and is recognized the world over. The Dutch fans wear replica shirts and other orange clothes to form a mass of color at games. Here, striker Klaas-Jan Huntelaar, nicknamed The Hunter, wears his national team's distinctive uniform.

WOOL SWEATERS
In the late 19th century, soccer jerseys were often made from wool. They tended to stretch out of shape and could become heavy in the rain because they soaked up water.

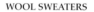

AWAY UNIFOR
In the 19
World C
final, t
England tea
wore cott
shirts wit
round col
Althou
England w
playing at hon
it did not wear t
normal white ho
strip because W
Germany wore whi
Players wo
red instea

LACE-UPS
At all levels of the game, teams began to wear matching uniforms. This black-and-white shirt was worn by a member of Newcastle United's team for the 1908 English FA Cup final. Newcastle still wears black-and-white today. The shirt is made of thick cotton with a lace-up collar. Lace-up collars became fashionable again in the 1990s and were worn by Manchester United, among other teams.

AUSTRALIAN AMATEURS
This Australian shirt is made from wool with a cotton collar. It was worn in 1925 by the player Tommy Traynor. Shirts worn in international games have symbolic importance. At the end of the game, the teams swap shirts with each other in a gesture of goodwill.

KEEPING COOL
Today, most shirts are designed to keep players cool and draw away excess moisture. This 1994 Brazil World Cup shirt is made of light, synthetic fabrics. With the energetic pace of modern games, such improvements are vital, especially for games played in hot climates.

FAIR-WEATHER FRIENDS
By the early 20th century, manufacturers in many countries had begun to adapt the gear that British players had taken overseas with them in the 19th century. They produced lighter outfits more suited to warm climates. Short-sleeved shirts and deep V-neck collars became part of the typical Mediterranean look, as represented on this image from Valencia in Spain.

Early 1900s Spanish illustration

These socks are unusually decorative

Women were not expected to head the ball

PULL UP YOUR SOCKS
These socks from the 1920s look just the same as modern ones but they are made of wool. Modern socks are made of synthetic materials, making them more comfortable. Players keep their socks up with ties around the top. The ties can be made from strips of bandage or elasticated tape cut up into lengths. Toward the end of a grueling game, when players are prone to cramps, they may discard the tie-ups. Socks around the ankle can be a tell-tale sign of a tired player facing defeat.

High kicking was easier if shorts were above the knees

Hoops and stripes are classic design features

Cream flannel shorts from about 1900

Modern synthetic shorts with decorative side seams

Hard-wearing cotton shorts from the 1930s

Early 20th-century French illustration

SHORT STORY
Amateurs in the 1860s played in full-length pants but, as the game developed, players had to increase their speed and agility. Shorter knickerbockers cut just above the knee became popular. The baggy style of soccer shorts of the 1930s was made famous by Alex James of Arsenal, England, "the wee man in the big shorts." This fashion was revived in the 1990s, following a trend in the 1970s and 1980s for tight shorts.

UNDER WRAPS
Until World War I, women players had to keep their hair under a cap or bonnet and hide their legs inside voluminous bloomers. In the 1910s, when many men were away at war, crowds flocked to see women's exhibition games. This wider acceptance of ladies' soccer enabled women's teams to start wearing soccer outfits that were similar to those worn by men and more suitable for the game.

Accessories

Catalog illustration of protective ear muffs

INJURY AND DISCOMFORT were part of the game of soccer in its early days. When protective equipment and other accessories, such as hats, ear muffs, and belts, were introduced at the end of the 19th century, they helped to distance the game from its rather violent past. Shin pads were developed in 1874 by Nottingham Forest's Samuel Widdowson in response to the physical punishment that players suffered during games. Leg protection is still part of gear today, but other accessories are no longer used.

Buttoned tunic was an alternative to the more common shirt

Leather buckles fasten these shin pads

LASTING DESIGN
In the 1900s, players would have worn shin pads like these outside their socks, held in place with straps and buckles. The front section is made of leather and the back of cotton, with a stuffing in between of animal hair. This mix of materials was used in shin pads until the 1960s.

THE FIRST SHIN PADS
The earliest shin pads were worn outside the socks and were extended to include ankle protectors, which rested on the top of the shoe. Some, like these, had a suede covering, which was more prone to water damage than other types of leather. These heavy and inflexible pads date from the 1890s, about 20 years after shin pads became part of the player's gear.

REINFORCED GUARDS
This figure is from a picture on the box of a late 19th-century German soccer game. His shin pads, worn over the top of his socks and knickerbockers, appear to be strengthened with cane bars.

BELT UP
Decorative belts were a part of many schoolboys' soccer gear until the 20th century. They neatened up appearances by holding in the shirt and gave teams identity through the use of colors. Belts were also part of women's gear in the early 1900s.

Early 20th-century schoolboys' belts

Woman's belt from 1895

1980s shin pads were similar in shape to those from the 1930s

Long laces to wrap twice around the leg

OM TO MOVE
1910, ankle protection was no longer t of shin pad design, not because it s not needed, but because it restricted vement of the foot. Passing and running the ball had become important parts of game, requiring increased flexibility he ankle. Players were therefore forced sacrifice some protection. Cork was netimes used to strengthen pads.

TIE-ON SHIN PADS
Shin pads worn inside the socks had taken over by 1930. Laces were used for fastening instead of buckles, to prevent chafing on the players' legs. Many years later, tighter-fitting synthetic, rather than woollen, socks held the pads firmly in position without the need for ties of any sort.

LIGHTWEIGHT PROTECTION
Modern shin pads look dramatically different from earlier models. They are shaped to fit the leg, using lightweight materials to give excellent protection. Even the delicate Achilles tendon at the back of the ankle is shielded. The revival of ankle protectors, after a gap of 100 years, brings shin pad design full circle.

Ladies wore hats to keep long hair out of the mud

Stripes to match team colors

Women's soccer hats

SOCCER FIGURINE
This porcelain figurine of a boy was made in Germany in the 1890s. Artistic depictions of soccer from this period often showed players wearing hats, even though they were becoming decorative rather than practical items.

Hand-painted German figurine

KEEPING WARM
Gloves have become common, especially among players from hot countries who play in Europe, often in freezing temperatures. Players susceptible to hamstring and groin injuries are encouraged to wear undershorts because they help to keep these important muscles warm.

Brazilian soccer player Gilberto Silva

HATS OFF!
These women's hats date from 1895, when ladies' soccer was still in its infancy. The fact that women played in hats does not mean that theirs was a gentler game. Like the men, many female players wore shin pads for protection.

Famous players

SOCCER IS A TEAM GAME. Clubs and national sides inspire the greatest passion among fans but a few players are so gifted and entertaining that they stand out from their teammates and draw thousands of extra people to games. Some great players are famous for their spirit of fair play, while others have been surrounded by controversy and bad publicity. But all of the great players share an ability to change the course of a game through a moment of incredible individual skill.

GORDON BANKS (b. 1937)
English goalkeeper Gordon Banks is remembered for one save in particular—a spectacular effort that kept out Pelé's header in the 1970 World Cup. Banks won 73 caps between 1963 and 1972 and would have won more, but for an eye injury.

JOHANN CRUYFF (b. 1947)
One of the few great players also to have become a successful manager, Cruyff was able to instill in his teams some of the style and tactical awareness that made him such a joy to watch. He played for Holland, Ajax, and Barcelona, Spain. He personified the concept of "total soccer" by floating all over the field and using his amazing balance and skill to open up defenses.

GERD MULLER (b. 1945)
Known as *"Der Bomber,"* Gerd Muller was an unlikely looking center-forward. He had an astonishing spring in his heels, which made up for his lack of height. He was a prolific goal scorer, with 68 goals in 62 games for West Germany. Most of his club soccer was played with Bayern Munich, Germany, for whom he scored a record 365 goals.

Milla was a great entertainer, known for his flamboyant goal celebrations

Roger Milla after scoring for Cameroon against Colombia in the 1990 World Cup

ROGER MILLA (b. 1952)
Twice African Player of the Year, Roger Milla of Cameroon was the first player to become famous worldwide playing for an African country. He was also the oldest player to appear and score in a World Cup match in 1994, aged 42.

BOBBY CHARLTON (b. 1937)
Manchester United star Bobby Charlton survived the Munich air crash that killed eight of his teammates in 1958. Known for the power and accuracy of his shooting, he was invaluable in England's 1966 World Cup win. He was knighted in 1994.

Eusébio practices ball control in training

DIEGO MARADONA (b. 1960)
Maradona was the best player of his generation and also one of the most controversial. He had a tremendous ability to inspire his teammates, most notably when leading Argentina to the 1986 World Cup and Napoli to two Series A titles in Italy in the late 1980s. His magical left foot and strength in possession were his main assets.

Maradona's low center of gravity gave him excellent balance

In the 1986 World Cup against England, Maradona scored two goals—one a handball that should have been disallowed, the other a dazzling solo effort

usébio scored
8 goals in 46
ternationals

USÉBIO (b. 1942)
though he was born in
ozambique, Eusébio was
apped up by Benfica of
sbon, Portugal, and went
to play for Portugal, in
mmon with several other
ented players. He starred
the 1962 European Cup
al, scoring twice as Benfica
at Real Madrid, Spain, 5–3.
usébio was respected all
er the world for his fair
ay and dignity as well as
his talent.

eazza (below right) shakes
ands with Hungarian
ptain, Sarosi, before the
938 World Cup Final

GARRINCHA (1933–83)
Nicknamed "the Little Bird," Garrincha had polio as a child. He overcame his disability to become one of the quickest and most elusive wingers the game has seen. He played on the right-hand side of Brazil's legendary 1958 forward line. In 1962, he made up for the absence of the injured Pelé with some brilliant performances, helping Brazil to retain the World Cup.

Like many of the greatest players, Maradona liked to be number 10

GIUSEPPE MEAZZA (1910–79)
Italian Giuseppe Meazza won two World Cup winner's medals in 1934 and 1938. He was respected as a creator and scorer of goals from his inside-forward position. In 1938, he organized the Italian team when the coach, Pozzo, was ordered to leave the bench and sit in the stands. He spent his best years at Internazionale of Milan, Italy, and won 53 caps.

Maradona's magical footwork entertained and amazed the fans

COUPE DU MONDE 1938

Continued on next page

MARCO VAN BASTEN (b. 1964)
Van Basten of Holland scored one of the greatest goals of all time at the European Championship final in 1988—a volley from wide of the goal. Sadly, an ankle injury cut short his career.

LUIS SUÁREZ (b. 1935)
Considered one of the best-ever Spanish players, Luis Suárez dominated the midfield for Barcelona, Spain, in the late 1950s. By the mid-1960s, he was playing a key part in Italian Inter Milan's new *catenaccio* system—a line-up heavy on defense with only two forward players. He was famous for his fast breaks out of defense and accurate passes. Suárez went on to be manager of Spain at the 1990 World Cup.

Kopa was the greatest French player of the 1950s

Kopa was known for his careful ball control and well-thought-out passing

Van Basten was the best center-forward of the late 1980s

RAYMOND KOPA (b. 1931)
Creative midfielder Raymond Kopa made his name with French club Reims. He led them to the first European Cup final in 1956, where they lost to Spain's Real Madrid. Kopa played for France at the 1958 World Cup and was named European Footballer of the Year in 1959.

The two defenders are playing for the Italian club Roma

Roma defenders are left in Platini's wake

STANLEY MATTHEWS (1915–2000)
England's Stanley Matthews was known for his dribbling skills. One of his finest performances was in Blackpool's 4–3 win over Bolton in the 1953 English FA Cup final. He won 84 caps and played his last game for Stoke City at the age of 50. He was knighted in 1965.

LEV YASHIN (1929–90)
Always dressed in black, Lev Yashin was rivaled only by Gordon Banks as the greatest goalkeeper of his era. He played for the Soviet Union in three World Cups and is, to this day, the only goalkeeper to have been named European Footballer of the Year.

Between them, Puskás and Di Stéfano scored seven goals in the European Cup final in 1960

FRANZ BECKENBAUER (b. 1945)
Beckenbauer's intelligence shone out on the field as he dictated play from a deep sweeper position. Together with Johann Cruyff, he is one of the few soccer-playing legends to achieve similar success as a manager. Having captained West Germany at the 1974 World Cup, he managed the team when it won again in 1990.

ENC PUSKÁS (1927–2006)
star of Hungary's famous team
he 1950s, Ferenc Puskás was
of the Hungarian team that
England 6–3 at Wembley in
3. He joined Real Madrid of
in 1958. Puskás strongly
red his left foot, scoring
ealth of stunning goals
both club
country.

ALFREDO DI STÉFANO (b. 1926)
When Real Madrid dominated European soccer in the 1950s, Di Stéfano was one of their star players. His stamina enabled him to contribute all over the field. He and Puskás formed one of soccer's legendary double acts.

HEL PLATINI (b. 1955)
ini was one of those
rs who seemed
py to take the
ght of a nation's
ectations on his
ulders. He captained
ce in the 1984 European
mpionships, and France
the tournament for
first time. Platini was
ttacking midfielder who
n finished as top scorer
alian club Juventus.

Michel Platini playing for Juventus

Platini had the speed and foresight to move forward into space

PELÉ (b. 1940)
Many people's choice of the greatest player of all, Pelé was king of Brazilian soccer from the late 1950s to the early 1970s. He overcame constant fouling by frustrated defenders to score more than 1,000 goals for Brazilian club Santos, American soccer team New York Cosmos, and the Brazilian national team. His enthusiasm and obvious love of playing, despite being plagued by injury, make him a perfect role model for the game of soccer.

Medals and caps

Sew-on badge given to members of an international squad

I**T IS THE GOAL OF ALL** soccer players to play well and win each game. Those lucky enough to win a championship are awarded a medal as a mark of their achievement. Those good enough to be picked to play for their country win a cap. Medals and caps have been part of the game since the 19th century and are still highly valued rewards today. At the highest level, success can be measured by the number of caps a player has and passing the "100 cap" mark is considered exceptional service to the national team. Thomas Ravelli of Sweden won 138 caps—a record for a European.

Argentine pot made from a dried eggplant trimmed with silver

Ornate silver dagger

Norwegian silver spoon

Argentine silver spoon

Medals

As with military medals for soldiers, soccer players are rewarded with medals for helping their side, not for a moment of personal glory. Medals are awarded at all levels of soccer, professional and amateur. They are mementos by which players can remember their glory days and can become valuable collectors' items.

GOOD SPORT
Before organized leagues were established, soccer medals were often awarded for sportsmanship as well as victories. The full-back C. Duckworth was given this medal for "gentlemanly and successful play" in the 1883–84 season.

WITH COMPLIMENTS
This "complimentary medal for defeating all comers" was awarded in the 1884–85 season.

PRECIOUS GIF
In addition to caps a medals, international play are sometimes presented with g by opposing soccer associations. T England team members each received a sil spoon when they faced Norway in 1949. T Argentine FA gave the English team memb ceremonial daggers and other silver items their first visit to Wembley, England, in 19

CLUB STRIKERS
Some clubs strike their own medals to mark a special achievement of their players. This medal was awarded at the end of a season to players of a team that had won its league.

Lancashire Cup winners 1887

English vs. Scottish League 1893

FA Cup runner-up 1893

DOUBLE
This group of medals belonged to R. H. Howarth of the Preston North End "Invincibles." The team won the League and the FA Cup in 1888–89, achieving the first English "double."

TROPHY TRIUMPH
This plaque was made to commemorate an international game between France and England in 1947. All the English players received a plaque after winning the match 3–0.

PLAYOFF PRIZES
Medals have been presented to the winners of the third and fourth place playoff match at every World Cup Final, except 1930 and 1950. In the World Cup Final in Germany 2006, the host nation won third place medals, defeating Portugal 3–1.

HUNGARY HIT
Hungary was one of the first continental European countries to take to soccer. It copied the way other countries organized the game, including the awarding of medals. This medal was awarded to the members of an international side after a game against Austria in 1909.

1909 Hungarian medal

CHAMPIONS
This medal was awarded to a player for success in the 1914–15 season.

AMATEUR
This 1920s medal was given to a successful amateur player.

ARSENAL STAR
This 1930s medal may have belong to soccer sta Alex James.

Caps

A colored cap was once the only way of showing to which side a player belonged. In 1872, the FA ruled that teams should wear distinctive shirts. In 1886, it was suggested that caps be awarded to players each time they played for their country. Today, they are given to every member of a national team, including playing substitutes. Often, only one cap is awarded for a series of games so a player with 50 "caps" may have fewer actual ones.

HOME CAP
This Welsh cap was awarded for the 1903–04 Home International games between England, Scotland, Northern Ireland, and Wales. This tournament took place every year until 1984.

CAREY'S CAP
The great defender Johnny Carey won his cap when he played for Ireland against Poland and Switzerland in 1938. Carey won 36 caps.

Tassels are added for decoration

Welsh national crest—a dragon

Details of games can be embroidered into each panel

Soccer caps are usually made from velvet

The date covers games from a whole season

Northern Ireland had its own team from 1921

SCHOOL COLORS
Soccer caps were first awarded in English private schools. "Colors," in the form of caps, were given to the most able players in each grade.

IN TRAINING
It is not only players that are rewarded for their efforts. Trainer Will Scott received this medal when the English and Scottish Leagues met at Celtic Park, Glasgow, Scotland, in November 1931.

WAR GAMES
Throughout World War II, famous international players took part in exhibition games arranged to boost public morale. In 1946, Tom Finney was given this set of three medals after appearing in a game in Antwerp, Belgium.

PROMOTIONAL MEDAL
By the 1950s, businesses had started to commemorate a range of soccer events. The French newspaper, *Le Soir*, made this medal to mark a club tour of Austria in 1953.

WORLD CUP
The biggest achievement in soccer is to win the World Cup. This is a spare Jules Rimet medal from the 1954 final, when West Germany beat the favorites, Hungary.

AFRICAN CUP
This medal was presented to the winners of the first African Nations' Cup in 1957. The competition was held in Khartoum, Sudan, and only Sudan, Ethiopia, and Egypt took part. Egypt beat Ethiopia 4–0 in the final.

Famous clubs

BRAVO BENFIC

Only Porto and Sporting Lisbon rival Benfica in th
Portuguese League. Benfica has also had som
notable victories on the more competiti
European stage. Benfica was the gre
team of the early 1960s, winning tw
European Cups, in 1961 and 196
and reaching but losing thre
further fina

ITALIAN ZEBRAS
Juventus is the most successful Italian club and enjoys great support outside Turin. Nicknamed the Zebras for their black-and-white striped uniform, they won the European Cup in 1985 and 1996.

Cᴌᴜʙs ɪɴsᴘɪʀᴇ the greatest loyalty and passion from soccer fans, more so even than national teams. In every country, certain big clubs attract followers from beyond their local areas and tend to dominate their domestic leagues and cups. Success for these clubs often continues because financial backing ensures a steady supply of good new players. In all corners of the world, people swear allegiance to Barcelona or Liverpool, Flamengo or Milan, although they may never be able to attend a game involving their team.

This bronze depicts Benfica's symbol, an eagle

Figure of the ancient Greek hero Ajax forms the basis of the Dutch club's crest

MIGHTY MARSEILLE
In 1993, Marseille, led by the attacking threat of Allen Boksic and Rudi Voller, beat AC Milan of Italy 1–0 to lift the European Cup. French administrators, such as long-time FIFA President Jules Rimet, have always had a large role in soccer, but it was 1993 before a French team won a European trophy.

LONDON LADIES
Netty Honeyball was the force behind the first great women's team in the 1890s. The British Ladies Club drew large crowds for its exhibition matches in London at a time when the capital was lagging behind the North and Midlands of England with regard to soccer.

YOUNG TALENT
In the 1970s, Dutch club Ajax's policy to develop its own young players bore fruit. The players, including the star Johann Cruyff, helped Ajax to three consecutive European Cup wins in the 1970s and some of them helped the national team in two World Cups. Despite regularly selling its best players, the club returned to the forefront of European soccer in the mid-1990s.

The club Ajax was formed in Amsterdam in 1900

BUSBY BABES
English club Manchester United started life as Newton Heath. It changed its name in 1902. The Munich air disaster of 1958, in which eight members of manager Matt Busby's young team died, inspired sympathy around the world. Since then, the club has won three European Cups—in 1968, 1999, and 2008.

Baines card from the 1890s shows fullback Jack Powell

PLAY UP NEWTON HEATH

POWELL

THE GOLDEN YEARS
Bayern Munich followed Ajax as the leading European team in the early 1970s. It won three consecutive European Cups with the help of players such as Franz Beckenbauer, Gerd Muller, and Sepp Maier, who were also important to the German national team.

Paul Breitner of Bayern Munich in 1974

Dominguez, the goalkeeper— from Argentina

Alfredo di Stéfano, the leader of the team

Francisco Gento, the fast left winger

REAL RIVALRY
In the late 1950s, Real Madrid, Spain, possibly had the greatest club side ever. Legends such as Di Stéfano and Puskás inspired this Spanish team to win the first five European Cups. Real Madrid has a spectacular stadium—the Bernabeu—and a bitter rivalry with Barcelona.

THE RED DEVILS
This picture shows the players Cagna and Rios of Independiente, Argentina, in 1995. In 1964, Independiente was the first Argentine club to win the South American club competition, the Copa Libertadores. The "Red Devils" went on to win the competition four more times between 1972 and 1975.

The fans

GONE BANANAS
In England in the late 1980s, there was a craze for taking large inflatables to games. Fans waved bananas, fish, and fried eggs in the crowd to show their support for their teams.

For all the talent displayed by the players on the field, it is the fans who have made soccer the biggest game in the world. From the last years of the 19th century, working people began to have enough free time to attend sporting events. They created an atmosphere of excitement and expectation, and large crowds became an important part of a game. Today, soccer is the most widely watched sport in the world. Fans are more eager than ever to show their support for club and country in a range of noisy and colorful ways.

Manchester City, England, pennant

Preston North End, England, rosette

PERFECT VIEW
In their desperation to see a game, fans are not always put off by the "ground full" signs. In the 19th century, before large-scale stands were built, trees provided a convenient spot from which to watch a popular game.

CLUB COLORS
Colors are a vital part of the bond between a team and its supporters. Once, people made rosettes for big matches and displayed pennants. Now, fans often wear a scarf to show their loyalty.

Holland scarf

Lazio, Italy, scarf

RARE COLLECTION
Fans have always collected objects bearing images of soccer. Today, the items probably feature their favorite club but, in the past, designs were based on more general soccer scenes. Collecting autographs is also a popular hobby and offers a rare opportunity to meet star players.

John "Jack" Rowley, forward

John Aston, fullback

Johnny Carey, fullback

Matt Busby, manager

Child's piggy bank

1950s autograph book containing signatures of famous figures of Manchester United, England

Wooden pencil case

During the war, the sound of the bell warned people of an air raid

Air-raid patrolman's rattle

Air-raid patrolman's bell

Adult's rattle

Rattles were originally used as bird scarers

Top section moves around and around horizontally

"Rattling" noise created at the handle

NOISY SUPPORT
Rattles were part of the atmosphere at games until the 1960s. When the horizontal section of the rattle is whirled around the "clicker" on the handle, it produces a loud rattling noise. Since the 1960s, organized chanting has become more common. Modern safety regulations restrict what items may be taken into the stadium, and rattles are no longer allowed.

Child's rattle

Child's rattle painted with a soccer scene

WAR CRY
Fans have taken bells and rattles to games to express their support since before 1940. This bell and rattle were part of an air-raid patrolman's equipment in England during World War II. In 1946, after the war, a Derby County fan took them to games during Derby's run-up to the English FA Cup final.

WORLD FAMOUS
Brazilian fans were famous for their noisy support long before the rest of the world discovered paints and drums. They produce a samba beat on their drums and blow their whistles. As the noise echoes around the stands, the fans dance to accompany the action, especially if their team is winning.

AFRICAN PAINTING
Face painting has become commonplace at major international games, adding to the color and spectacle of the occasion. Here, two Zambian fans, painted to reflect the team's colors, enjoy an African Nations Cup match. Face painting is particularly popular with Dutch, Danish, and Japanese fans.

Game day

This is a scoreboard from an early 20th-century French soccer game

THE ATMOSPHERE of a big game, the sound of the crowd, and the closeness of the players combine to make going to a live soccer game very addictive. Even though soccer is now widely shown on television, millions of fans still go to the games. Many supporters, like players, are extremely superstitious and follow the same routine every time they go to a game. The crowd and the noisy support they give their team are essential to the game of soccer. It is vital that clubs continue to improve comfort and safety for their fans, so that they keep on coming back.

ALL DRESSED UP
This photo shows fans of West Ham, England, preparing to travel to the 1923 FA Cup final, the first to be held at Wembley. Many more than the official attendance of 123,000 crammed into the stadium. Notice the stylish appearance of the fans.

In the 1988 European Championship final, Holland beat the Soviet Union 2–0

Holograms and complicated designs are now used to deter ticket forgeries

TICKETS, PLEASE
Tickets are essential in controlling access to games and keeping attendance to a safe level. Years ago, this was only necessary at cup finals and World Cup games. Tickets were issued for general areas in the stadium. Now that general seating has been phased out in favor of ticketed seating, each ticket corresponds to a particular seat.

READING MATTER
The earliest programs were simple one-sheet items, giving only team line-ups. As soccer became more popular, further elements were added, such as a message from the manager and background information on the opposition. Glossy, full-color brochures, largely paid for by advertising, are produced for tournaments such as the European Championships.

LET ME ENTERTAIN YOU
To make going to a game even more enjoyable, particularly for a family audience, clubs and governing bodies put on extra entertainment before kickoff and at halftime. In the past, this may have taken the form of a brass band, but modern crowds expect something more elaborate. The opening ceremony at the World Cup Finals in Germany in 2006 featured Bavarian drummers and dancers lowered from the roof to the field.

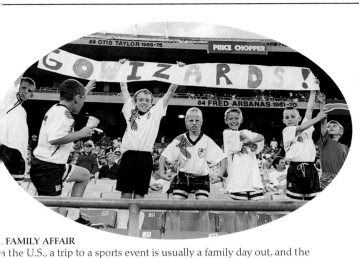

FAMILY AFFAIR
In the U.S., a trip to a sports event is usually a family day out, and the stadiums have good facilities for everyone. There is a lot of razzmatazz at the Major League Soccer games. Cheerleaders and music keep the crowds well entertained. This is game day at the Kansas City Wizards' stadium.

1903 FA official's badge

Official badge from 1905

The badges are made of cloth and decorated with gold brocade

FA badge from 1898

The English three lions motif

Badge worn at 1899 England vs. Scotland international

ACCESS ALL AREAS?
Away from the mass of spectators, there are certain areas of the stadium, such as the boardroom, where access is strictly controlled. These badges, from 1898–1905, would have been sewn on blazers and worn by Football Association officials. These days, executive boxes have become a feature at many stadiums.

CROWD CONTROL
Police and guards attend soccer games to ensure the safety of everyone at the game. Police, like these Italian officers at a Juventus game, may need to take a hard line with unruly fans, and sometimes use horses or dogs to help them control large crowds. They may also control traffic and escort fans to and from the game.

COMING HOME
This drawing comes from a postcard from the early 20th century. The caption on the card says, "Our team's lost by ….. goals to …..". Space is left on the card for fans to fill in the score. Somehow, the depression of defeat is always replaced by excitement and high hopes when the next game comes around.

The stadium

As CROWDS GREW EVER larger in the late 19th century, soccer clubs realized that they would have to build somewhere permanent to hold their games. Stadiums became a necessity. They provided fans with shelter and a decent view of the game. They also created an atmosphere that added greatly to the game-day experience. A series of stadium disasters over the years, in places such as Scotland, Peru, and Russia, finally led to the widespread belief that open seating should be replaced by stands for the safety of spectators.

SHEFFIELD WEDNESDAY F.C.

THEN THERE WAS LIGHT...
Floodlights were first used in 1878 but they did not become standard at professional clubs until the 1950s. The most common form of stadium lighting was on tall towers in the corners of the stadium. Today, lights are often placed in rows along the stand roof.

CROWD SAFETY
On April 15, 1989, the FA Cup semifinal at Hillsborough, Sheffield, was the scene of the worst disaster in English soccer history. Ninety-six Liverpool fans died as a result of a crowd crush. The report into the tragedy began a major leap forward in stadium safety, to prevent a similar disaster from ever happening again.

STATE OF THE ART
The new Wembley Stadium in north London took much longer than anticipated to erect and construction costs were considerably higher than initial estimates. Once it opened, however, the public flocked to this stunning stadium with its 90,000 capacity and giant screens, each the size of 600 television sets. The stadium boasts a fantastic steel arch that is lit up at night and can be seen all across the city.

Lights along the top of the roof

STANDING TALLER
Barcelona, Spain, moved from Les Corts Stadium to the spectacular Nou Camp in 1957. Improvements for the 1982 World Cup and 1992 Olympics have increased the staggering height of the stands. The Nou Camp was paid for by the club's members.

PATH TO THE FIELD
The tunnel is more than just a route on to the field. It is the place where players psych themselves up for the game and give in to their superstitions. Many insist on taking the same place in the line every time. Others put on their shirts only at the last moment.

The roof "hangs" from this crossbar

The tower is integral to the structure of the stand

KEEPING UP TO DATE
Modern stands are designed using computer models to ensure that everybody has a good view. The space between seats is a difficult issue. More space means greater comfort, but it reduces the capacity of the stand. Designs, such as faces, are often picked out in the seats.

FANS ON THEIR FEET
Before seating in stadiums was introduced, fans stood packed together in areas of open admission. Far more fans could get in to watch a game and it is how the majority of people have watched games for much of soccer's history. Children were often passed over the heads of the crowd to the front to give them a better view.

WORLD CUP WONDER
The Stade de France is in St. Denis, north of Paris. It was built for the 1998 World Cup and 80,000 spectators watched the opening game there between Brazil and Scotland. The stadium was widely praised for its dramatic design. The roof, enclosing the ground in a continuous curve, creates an amphitheater effect, which has always been popular in European and South American stadiums.

several tiers of seats

Field-level openings for emergency vehicles

Revolving advertising billboards around the field

45

The World Cup

THE SOCCER WORLD CUP is one of the greatest sporting events of our time. The first World Cup was held in Uruguay in 1930, 26 years after FIFA first discussed the idea. In the early days, some teams were unable to travel to the host country but, by the 1950s, long-distance travel was becoming much easier and quicker. As the tournament became more accessible, it grew in popularity. The 1950 World Cup Final at the Maracana Stadium in Rio de Janeiro was attended by 200,000 people.

In 1958, Brazilian teenager Pelé became the first global soccer superstar. Since then, interest in the World Cup has boomed.

MANY MASCOTS
Every World Cup since 1966 has had a mascot. They appear as a life-size figure at games and scaled-down promotional or commercial images. This is Pique, from Mexico '86.

WORLD FIRST
Uruguay offered to pay travel and accommodation expenses to the 13 visiting teams at the first World Cup. Only four European teams made the long journey, joining the seven South American teams.

1954—Switzerland. West Germany beat Hungary 3–2 in one of the great upsets in World Cup history.

1958—Sweden. Brazil beat Sweden 5–2. Brazil is the only team to have played in every Finals tournament.

1950—Brazil. Uruguay beat Brazil 2–1, in the first tournament after World War II.

1962—Chile. Brazil beat Czechoslovakia 3–1, with Garrincha taking center stage after Pelé was injured.

1938—France. Italy beat Hungary 4–2, inspired by its star inside-forward, Meazza.

1966—England. West Germany lost 2–4 to England in extra time, with Geoff Hurst scoring the first hat trick in a final.

1934—Italy. Czechoslovakia lost 1–2 to Italy. Uruguay did not defend its crown, the only time this has happened.

1970—Mexico. Brazil beat Italy 4–1 and was one of the greatest teams of all time.

1930—Uruguay. Beating Argentina 4–2, Uruguay was the first of many host countries to win the Cup.

1974—West Germany. Holland was beaten 2–1 by West Germany, which came back from being a goal behind.

VARIOUS VENUES
Competition to stage the World Cup Finals is always fierce because it brings visitors and publicity to the host country. The 2002 Finals, in Japan and South Korea, were the first shared tournament. In 2006, the Finals were held in Germany. The 2010 host is South Africa.

Argentina '78 is remembered for the ticker tape in the River Plate Stadium

Mexico was the first country to host two Finals

The Italia '90 mascot was called Ciao

1978—Argentina. Holland lost 1–3 to Argentina, leaving the Dutch as the best team never to have won the World Cup.

1982—Spain. Italy beat West Germany 3–1, its striker Paolo Rossi finishing as leading scorer.

1986—Mexico. Argentina beat West Germany 3–2, in a tournament dominated by Diego Maradona.

1990—Italy. West Germany beat Argentina 1–0 in a defensive, bad-tempered final.

1998—France. Brazil was beaten 3–0 by France in an amazingly one-sided game.

1994—USA. Brazil beat Italy 3–2 on penalties after a 0–0 draw and became the only team to have won four World Cups.

In 1994, American fans turned out in force to watch the games

The fans at Italia '90 provided more drama than some of the games

The figure is a winged seraph

WANDERING TROPHY

The first World Cup trophy was designed by a French sculptor, Abel Lafleur. Originally named "Victory," it was later named in honor of the president of FIFA, Jules Rimet. The trophy was stolen before the 1966 tournament in England and was found in a park by a dog named Pickles. Brazil was presented with the trophy to keep in 1970 but, in 1983, it was stolen again and has not been seen since.

The engraving on the trophy is in French

The trophy is made of solid gold

Sweden, the host team, made it to the final in 1958 but was overpowered by the Brazilian superteam

COUPE DU MONDE DE FOOTBALL ASSOCIATION COUPE JULES RIMET

Jules Rimet trophy

READ ALL ABOUT IT

Programs for the World Cup are different from the club variety, in that they usually cover the whole tournament rather than a specific game. They contain information about the competing teams and are printed in several languages. These programs are from Sweden '58, England '66, Spain '82, Italy '90, and USA '94.

Didi

Pelé was 17 in 1958

Garrincha

Vava played at center-forward

Zagalo, the left-winger, scored the fourth goal in the final

THE BEAUTIFUL GAME

The 1958 final saw Brazil emerge as one of the World Cup's greatest-ever teams. Their forward line-up was among the strongest in the game's history. Garrincha, Didi, Vava, Pelé, and Zagalo drove the team to victory. Mario Zagalo later became the national team manager and was in charge when Brazil won again in 1970 and 1994.

Continued on next page

Continued from previous page

WE MUST HAVE THE WORLD CUP

This was the poster for the 1962 Finals in Chile. A series of earthquakes marred the run-up to the tournament but the hosts were determined. President of the Chilean FA, Carlos Dittborn, said "We have nothing. That is why we must have the World Cup." Chile overcame the doubts of some European teams by staging a successful event. There was more trouble on the field than off it, particularly in the "Battle of Santiago" between Italy and Chile. Italy finished the game with nine men.

CAMPEONATO MUNDIAL DE FUTBOL
WORLD FOOTBALL CHAMPIONSHIP
CHAMPIONNAT MONDIAL DE FOOTBALL
COUPE JULES RIMET
CHILE 1962

Globe forms the top of the trophy

World Cup Willie inspired a World Cup theme song by Lonnie Donegan

The Union Jack flag represents Great Britain, not just England

WORLD CUP

The real trophy is 20 in (50.8 cm) high and weighs 20 lbs (9 kg)

Designed by Italian Silvio Gazzaniga, the trophy is made of solid 18-carat gold

World Cup Willie was a lion, inspired by the three lions on the England gear

Replica of the World Cup trophy

MASCOTS FOR MONEY

World Cup Willie was the first World Cup mascot. Designed for the 1966 tournament in England, he represented the increase in commercialism. Since then, tournament mascots, such as Footix of France 1998 and Zakumi of South Africa 2010, have appeared on official posters and been sold in many forms.

NEW LOOK CUP

The present World Cup trophy was made for the 1974 Finals in West Germany. Having won for the third time in 1970, Brazil had been allowed to keep the Jules Rimet trophy for good. The new trophy was commissioned by FIFA, despite an offer from Brazil to provide a trophy named after FIFA president, Sir Stanley Rous.

LIMITED EDITION OF THE PRESEN

THINKING POSITIVELY

In 1978, hosts Argentina inspired passionate fans with its positive attitude. The star of its winning team was Mario Kempes, who played club soccer in Europe.

Enter
GATE SEC ROW SEAT
F 222 11 4

Tuesday, June 28, 1994
R.F.K. Stadium

12:30 pm Kickoff

XV FIFA World Cup

GAME
30

ITA vs MEX

$37.50   Category 2

WILLIAM SMART

Washington, D.C.

WorldCupUSA**94**

© 1991 WC'94 TM

0 0 0 0 0 0 0 0 0 0 0 0 0

SEE REVERSE SIDE FOR TERMS AND CONDITIONS

ENTHUSIASTIC AMERICA

Despite having no strong tradition of professional soccer, the US hosted a successful World Cup Final in 1994. Large and enthusiastic crowds attended all the games. This is a ticket for the game between Italy and Mexico, played at the former RFK Stadium, now the Jack Kent Cooke Stadium, home to football team the Washington Redskins.

Information pack for Spain 1982

Spanish Football Federation crest

A pack of cards illustrating the stadiums

HARD WORK FOR HOSTS

A country bids to hold the World Cup several years in advance. It tries to convince FIFA that it will be able to stage a successful tournament. It has to produce information about all aspects of the tournament, including the stadiums, transportation networks, accommodation, and media facilities. South Africa's bid to host the 2010 World Cup finals was successful, making it the first African nation to stage the competition.

The balls are brightly colored for the benefit of TV audiences

Each ball contains a slip of paper with a team written on it

WHO PLAYS WHOM?

Plastic balls like these are used to make the draw for the World Cup Finals. It is a fair way to decide who plays whom. The number of competing teams has steadily increased from 13 in 1930 to 32 in 2010. The present system ensures that every team gets to play three games in the first round. Then, for the rest of the tournament, games are played on a knock-out basis, until only two remain for the grand final.

IN THE BAG

This bag is a promotional item for the 2002 World Cup, staged jointly by Japan and South Korea. It was the first shared tournament and the first one held in Asia. Demand is sure to increase for smaller countries to benefit from this arrangement.

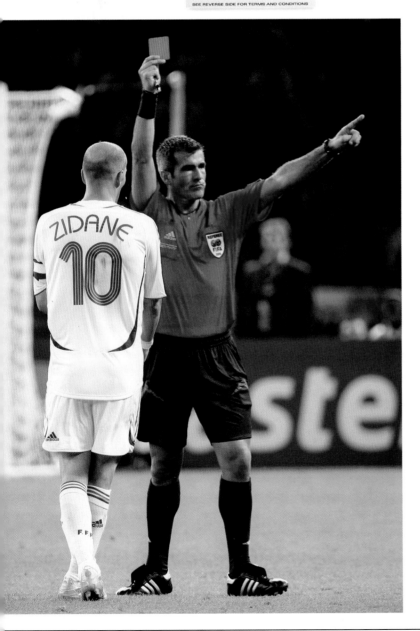

ZIDANE SEES RED

The defining moment of the 2006 World Cup Final came when referee Orazio Elizondo sent off French captain Zinédine Zidane after his infamous head-butt of Italian defender Marco Matarazzi. With the score at 0–0 after overtime, Italy went on to win the game on penalties.

Cups and trophies

THE MOMENT WHEN a team captain is presented with a trophy and holds it up to the fans is the crowning glory of any campaign. Cups and trophies are the marks of success and the managers of many modern clubs know that, if they are to hold on to their job, their team has to win a competition. For clubs like Real Madrid in Spain, Benfica in Portugal, and Bayern Munich in Germany, finishing as runner-up is considered a failure. The desire to make money has led to the creation of many new competitions in recent years, some of which do not have the same prestige as older tournaments such as the European Cup or the Copa America.

OLYMPIC SOCCER
This pin is from the 1956 Olympic Games. The Olympics featured demonstration soccer games from 1896. The first proper Olympic tournament was in 1908.

TEAM TALK
The European Cup was originally for the champions of each country's league. Now the top two clubs compete. The competition was first held in 1956. At the 1985 final at the Heysel Stadium in Brussels, Belgium, 39 people died. A safety wall collapsed as fans of Juventus, Italy, and Liverpool, England, fought each other.

Program for the 1985 European Cup final

Corner flags used as decoration

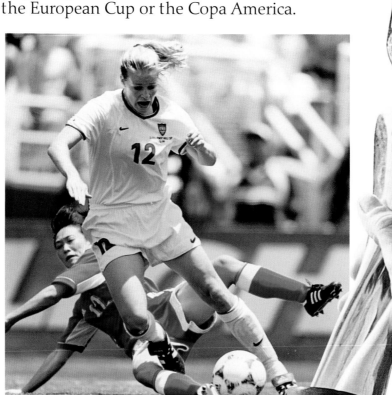

The gold-plated Women's World Cup trophy has a soccer ball on top

Holding the trophy aloft is a proud moment

FULL HOUSE
In the 1999 Women's World Cup in the US, teams played in front of capacity crowds. The final was held in the Rose Bowl in Pasadena, California. Here, US player Cindy Parlow rides a tackle in the final against China. The US won, to secure its second World Cup victory.

WOMEN'S WORLD CUP
The first Women's World Cup took place in China in 1991. The final was held in Guangzhou, where the US beat Norway 2–1. The tournament went from strength to strength and the next two events, in 1995 and 1999, drew large crowds. This is the trophy awarded to the US in 1999.

EARLY CUP
This decorative, silver-plated trophy from the 1870s is an example of an early soccer cup. After the FA Cup was started in 1872, local tournaments for small clubs began to be set up all over England and Scotland along the same lines.

PLAYER'S CIGARETTES

PLAYER'S CIGARETTES

ASSOCIATION CUP WINNERS
THE OLD CUP

ASSOCIATION CUP W...
THE PRESENT CU...

LITTLE TIN IDOLS
The first FA Cup, on the left, was known as the Little Tin Idol. It was stolen from a store window in 1895 and was never recovered. The present FA Cup, on the right, was made in Bradford, England, in 1911.

The silver UEFA trophy is decorated with men playing soccer

Names of previous winners engraved around the base

FROM STRENGTH TO STRENGTH
The African Nations Cup has been held every two years since 1957. It has grown from humble beginnings and as many as 16 teams now take part. Egypt captain Ahmed Hassan is pictured here in 2008 after his team's 1–0 win over Cameroon. This was Egypt's sixth African Nations title.

The Copa America was conceived by Chile, Uruguay, Brazil, and Argentina

COPA AMERICA CUP
First held in 1910, the Copa America is the oldest major international competition. It was originally played for only by South American countries but, in recent years, Mexico and the US have also taken part. Uruguay won the first official Copa America in 1917 and, along with Argentina, has been the most successful over the years. Brazil has not always played its strongest team. Since 1987, the tournament has been held every two years.

SECOND BEST
The UEFA (Union of European Football Associations) Cup was originally known as the Inter City Fairs Cup. The first competition was played over three years, beginning in 1955. Barcelona beat London 8–2 in the two-legged final. When the European Cup Winners' Cup was abolished in 1999, only two European club competitions remained. The strongest sides qualify for the European Cup and the next best play in the UEFA Cup. From 2009/10 the UEFA Cup became known as the Europa League and included a group stage similar to the Champions League.

Playing the game

GENERATIONS OF children have had their first contact with soccer, or "football," through toys such as blow soccer, card games, and Subbuteo. The popularity of soccer means that, as with other merchandise, there is money to be made from developing new products with a soccer theme. This drives manufacturers and inventors to come up with a vast range of games based on soccer, far more than on any other sport. The simplicity of the toys from the past, shown here, contrasts sharply with the speed and excitement of modern computer games. Today, people can experience virtual soccer games and act out the roles of their favorite players and teams on games consoles.

Two lead "kicking" figurines from the early 20th century

This game was advanced for its time

Points are lost if a marble is trapped here

Marbles are fired up this chute

PIN FOOTBALL.

ORDERED OFF-FIELD
BALL LOST

FREE KICK 50   FOUL (MINUS) 25   THROW IN 25

GOOD SHOT 90   GOOD PASS 75

PENALTY KICK 150

CENTRE 100

FOG   CORNER 75   CORNER 75   GOAL KICK 5

GOAL 200

ALL LOST BALLS RETURNED

MADE IN KAY ENGLAND

TRENCH GOAL FOOTBALL
BRITISH DESIGN   BRITISH MADE

KICK OFF   REGISTRATION APPLIED FOR

BALL ROLLING
This handheld toy was made in the early 20th century. It involves rolling the ball-bearing into one of the small holes.

IN THE TRENCHES
Trench Soccer was produced for British soldiers fighting in World War I. The player must move a ball-bearing safely past the German generals to score.

SOCCER MATCHBOX
This is the world's smallest soccer game, probably made in Japan in the 1930s for young children. When the matchbox is opened, a spring is released and the players leap up.

PINBALL
In this bagatelle game from the 1950s, players shoot marbles around the board using a spring in the bottom right-hand corner. Points are scored or lost according to where the marbles stop.

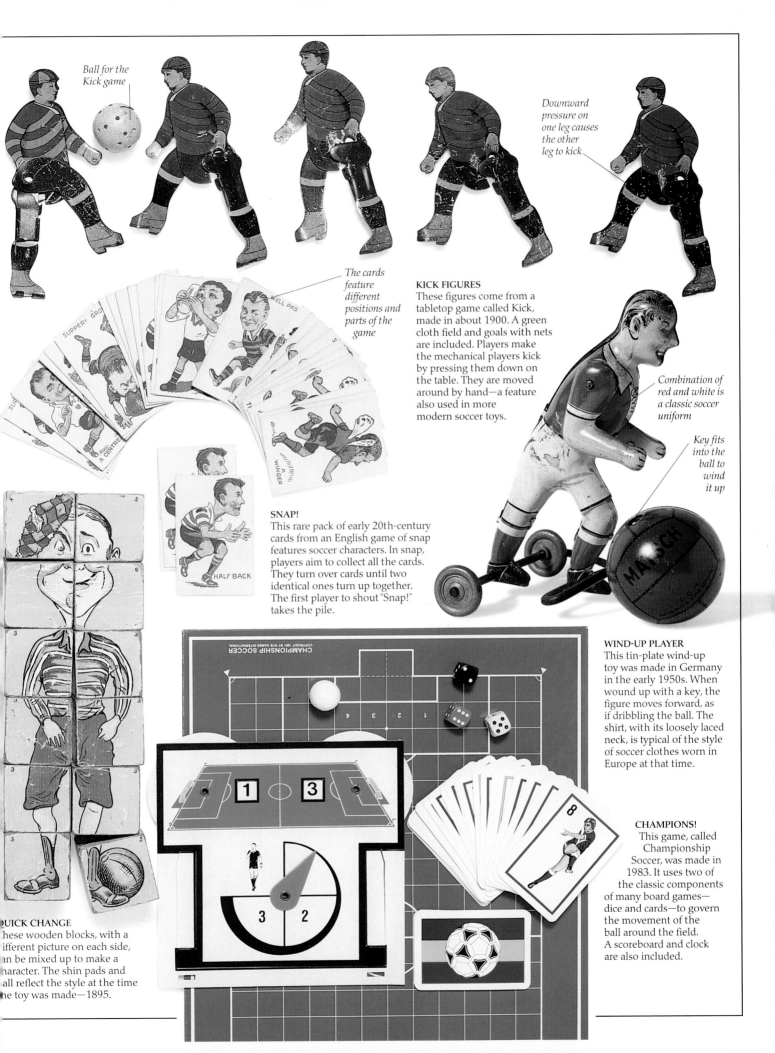

Ball for the Kick game

Downward pressure on one leg causes the other leg to kick

The cards feature different positions and parts of the game

KICK FIGURES
These figures come from a tabletop game called Kick, made in about 1900. A green cloth field and goals with nets are included. Players make the mechanical players kick by pressing them down on the table. They are moved around by hand—a feature also used in more modern soccer toys.

Combination of red and white is a classic soccer uniform

Key fits into the ball to wind it up

SNAP!
This rare pack of early 20th-century cards from an English game of snap features soccer characters. In snap, players aim to collect all the cards. They turn over cards until two identical ones turn up together. The first player to shout "Snap!" takes the pile.

WIND-UP PLAYER
This tin-plate wind-up toy was made in Germany in the early 1950s. When wound up with a key, the figure moves forward, as if dribbling the ball. The shirt, with its loosely laced neck, is typical of the style of soccer clothes worn in Europe at that time.

CHAMPIONS!
This game, called Championship Soccer, was made in 1983. It uses two of the classic components of many board games— dice and cards—to govern the movement of the ball around the field. A scoreboard and clock are also included.

QUICK CHANGE
These wooden blocks, with a different picture on each side, can be mixed up to make a character. The shin pads and ball reflect the style at the time the toy was made—1895.

Memorabilia

SOCCER appeals to all parts of the community, regardless of age or sex. The game can therefore be used to promote a wide range of items. Soccer-related advertising and product promotion is not a new phenomenon. In fact, companies were already latching on to the game's popularity in the early part of the 20th century. An understated style and original artwork predominated until the 1950s. This has been largely replaced today by mass-produced items, heavily reliant on star players and wealthy clubs.

1910 silver Vesta (match holder) advertising the mustard maker Colman's

Bank Top White Star

Wednesday, now Sheffield Wednesday

Welsh national team

Chadderton, a non-league team

Scottish club, Hearts

BAINES CARDS
These cards, produced in the late 19th and early 20th century, were the forerunners of sticker albums and other collectibles. They featured soccer and rugby league teams at professional and amateur level and had advertisements on the reverse side.

SPORTS TIN
By the 1930s, original artwork on a sporting theme was often used as a decoration for everyday household items. This tin features soccer on the lid and other sports, including cricket and hockey, around the outside.

Covered stands are rare in southern Europe

POSTER PAINTING
In this advertising card of the 1920s, an Italian drinks company has illustrated its product in a soccer scene, instead of putting a soccer image on the actual bottle.

This label comes from a fruity soft drink. It was marketed as an ideal refreshment for half-time

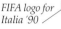

FIFA logo for Italia '90

SOUVENIRS
Mementos of the World Cup Finals do not stop at programs and tickets. There is great demand around the world for anything tied to the tournament, such as these erasers from Italia '90.

FOOTBALL FAN
This is a Spanish lady's fan from the mid-20th century, printed in Barcelona. It has a soccer image on one side and carries a promotional message on the reverse. Many commercial objects of this period were designed to be artistic as well as functional.

HEALTHY KICK
There is no magic ingredient in this drink, but the images would have appealed to soccer fans. The manufacturers knew that any association with soccer would improve sales.

This label implies that the drink will promote the robust strength that a soccer player enjoys

Banks Johnstone Jennings England Best

Class B17 locomotive

TEAM TRAIN
In the early 1980s, the Hornby toy company of Liverpool, England, produced a series of these scale models of the London North Eastern Railway's locomotives, named after soccer clubs. This one is called the *Manchester United*. Real trains are also sometimes named after clubs.

Name plate

The kicking leg is the second hand

HEADS IT IS
The Cleveland Petrol company produced these miniatures of British international players in 1971. The set was given away free with gasoline sales.

Pocket watch

Watch

Alarm clock

FULL TIME
This group includes a Swiss pocket watch made in Geneva around 1910, a British watch from the 1950s, and a more modern 1970s alarm clock. Design, materials, and therefore cost, were dictated by whether the object was aimed at children or adults.

Chain

CHAIN MEDALS
Soccer items are often turned into jewelry and other personal effects. Four silver medals, struck in the 1920s, are attached to this chain. The silver locket and compass are from the 1880s.

Locket

Compass

Further medals could be added to the chain

OLYMPIC CLOCK
This German wooden clock may well have been made to commemorate the 1936 Berlin Olympics, where the soccer tournament was won by Italy, when it beat Austria 2–1 in the final. The figures at the top of the clock move on the hour.

The figure is the same on both halves

CHOCOLATE
Melted chocolate would have been poured into this early 20th-century brass mold and left to cool and set, producing a miniature chocolate player with a ball at his feet. This item was made to appeal mainly to children and the general soccer theme would have been enough to make it popular.

SOAP ON A ROPE
The Avon company produced this soap soccer ball to mark the 1966 World Cup Final in England.

STRING ALONG
Made in the 1880s, this copper string holder prevents string from getting tangled. The string is pulled through a hole in the top.

The business of soccer

SOCCER IS BIG BUSINESS—fans attend games in large numbers, club products sell worldwide, and top players and managers earn incredibly large salaries. The clubs and professional players of the 1880s realized the financial possibilities of soccer but, for many decades, the game carried on at much the same level. It provided cheap entertainment for the paying public and offered a decent living to players and managers. All that has changed now, as club owners and star players stretch soccer's money-making potential to the limit.

BILLY'S BRIBE
This shirt was worn by Welshman Billy Meredith, the greatest player of his era. As a player for Manchester City, England, he was banned from playing for a year in 1905. He allegedly tried to bribe the Aston Villa captain to lose an important game. This was the first major scandal of British soccer.

Romário is pictured here playing in Vasco de Gama's white home shirt with trademark diagonal black stripe

The company logo of the club's gear sponsors is displayed in the center of the shirt

Even shin pads, worn under the socks, are marked with the name of the manufacturer

SHIRTS OFF
Replica shirts are a major source of income for professional clubs like England's Manchester United and Spain's Real Madrid. Three or four designs are available at one time and new ones are brought out at regular intervals. Clubs produce hundreds of different products— from calendars to baby clothes; from candy to bicycles. These can be sold to fans all over the world, reducing the club's reliance on ticket receipts.

MANAGEMENT STRESS
Managers are subjected to great stress in the modern game and have to accept that their every decision will be examined by the media. In most of the major leagues, the length of time allowed for a manager to produce a winning team can be measured in months rather than years. In 2007, Brazilian star Romário became player-manager of Vasco da Gama. He scored three times for the club during his stint as manager.

SHIRT AD
Companies have been paying soccer clubs to put their logos on their shirts since the 1970s. The only club not to have a sponsor's logo has been the Spanish club Barcelona. In 2006, the club carried the emblem of UNICEF—the United Nations Children's Fund—for free.

Strikers, such as Ronaldo, fetch the highest prices

GROUND FORCE

Advertising in and around soccer grounds was allowed long before shirt sponsorship. In the 1950s, it featured mainly local firms, but now larger multinational companies exploit the exposure provided by television coverage. Some billboards rotate, to catch the eye of the viewing public and allow more advertisers to use limited space. In some competitions, such as the European Champions' League, the same products are advertised at every game in the tournament.

RONALDO'S RECORD

layers today are eager to change ubs regularly because of the gning bonuses they receive. ices have continued to yrocket in recent years, th a new record set 2009 by Portugal's ristiano Ronaldo. e superstar alscorer became e most expensive ayer in soccer story when he moved om Manchester United to al Madrid for a staggering e of $128 million.

L ABROAD!

litical and legal changes have ade it easy for players to move road and play for foreign clubs. ropean Union (EU) residents n play in any member ate, while players from n-EU countries must eet specified criteria go abroad. Players m overseas, ch as Ghanian dfielder Michael sien, are now in e majority at e Premiership bs of gland.

Ghana's Michael Essien moved from French club Lyon to English side Chelsea

Pin showing AC Milan's club logo

MEDIA MOGULS

AC Milan is one of the many teams with links to big business. Italian media mogul Silvio Berlusconi bought the club at a time when television coverage of the game was increasing. He was able to maximize commercial opportunities and attract star players from abroad.

World Club Cup

WORLD CHAMPIONS

The World Club Cup is contested by the winners of the UEFA Champions League and the Copa Libertadores. The first competition was between Real Madrid, Spain, and Penarol, Uruguay, in 1960. Originally, a home-and-away fixture, won by the team with the highest aggregate score, it was changed in 1980 to one game only, played in Japan.

The science of soccer

FOR MANY YEARS, SOCCER was not considered a subject of scientific investigation and coaches and players relied largely on knowledge gained from experience. As technology has become more sophisticated, and the difference between winning and losing smaller, ways of using science to improve soccer have been developed. Nutritionists have transformed players' diets, physicists have studied how and why some players can bend the ball, and information technology has made a statistical analysis of the game possible.

BIOLOGICAL DIFFERENCES
For much of the first century of soccer, women were marginalized on the grounds that they were physically unsuited to the game. However, as the Brazilian player Milene Dominguez shows here, women have all the touch and skills of men, if not the sheer bulk and strength.

ISOTONIC NUTRITION
Players can lose up to seven pints (3 liters) of water during a game so it is imperative that they rehydrate their bodies during and after a match. Isotonic drinks, which contain a small amount of salts and sugars, are the most effective for doing this. The drinks also help replenish the player's stock of calories.

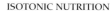

German players exercise their abductor muscles, which lift the leg outward from the body

Players run around poles to test their capacity to change direction at speed

With one foot off the ground, turning on the run, players develop their sense of balance

TRAINING MUSCLES
Training was once little more than a few laps around the field, but today advances in medical science have resulted in highly specialized regimes. Players warm up and warm down to prevent muscle strain and do specific work on individual muscles to help them cope with the range of moves needed during the game.

PHYSICAL DEMANDS
The German national team was put through its paces before the 2006 World Cup, its levels of fitness monitored and recorded in training exercises like this.

A microchip inside the ball will determine whether the ball crossed the line

A CLEVER LITTLE CHIP
Did all of the ball cross all of the line? It is a question referees, players, and fans are always arguing over. The insertion of a microchip into this foam-stuffed ball, combined with field-side tracking devices, may one day provide a definitive answer.

⟵ Direction of attack

Distance covered: 5478

PROZONE
Software such as Prozone can track the precise movements of players in a game, re-create passages of play in animated form, and provide incredibly detailed statistics. This screen shows the movements of a central midfielder over one half of a game. The dot in the center shows the player's average position on the field, while the distance the player has run is calculated at more than 3 miles (5 km).

FLAGS THAT GO BLEEP
Assistant referees are now equipped with blip flags. If something has been missed, especially incidents off the ball, the assistant can alert the referee by pressing a button on the flag's handle. The referee's receiver, strapped to their arm, will then vibrate or bleep.

The muscles in a player's leg have to learn to switch rapidly from relaxed to contracted and back again

Flags with blip buttons like this were first introduced in the late 1990s

Did you know?

AMAZING FACTS

A three-minute egg

⚽ On average, each player in a game has the ball for only three minutes, the time it takes to boil an egg!

⚽ In 1965, substitutes were allowed for the first time, but only when a player was injured. Substitutes featured in the World Cup for the first time in 1970.

⚽ Johann Cruyff's mother was a cleaner for the club Ajax in Holland. When she persuaded them to give her 10-year-old son a trial, they signed him as a youth player. He went on to be an international soccer star.

⚽ The goal net only became compulsory in 1892. The crossbar was introduced in 1875.

⚽ The first time teams used numbered shirts in an FA Cup final was in 1933. Everton wore numbers 1 to 11, and Manchester City wore numbers 12 to 22.

⚽ Eight of the players who won the World Cup for Brazil in 1958 were in the team that retained the World Cup in 1962.

⚽ Only seven different countries have been World Cup champions, although there have been 18 finals.

⚽ The FA Cup is the oldest competition in soccer. The highest scoring FA Cup victory was on October 15, 1887, when Preston North End beat Hyde United 26–0 in the first round of the competition. The score was 12–0 at half-time and 25–0 at 90 minutes. The final goal was scored in the five minutes of extra time added by the referee.

⚽ Pelé scored 1,283 goals during his senior career.

⚽ Half of the world's registered soccer players are from Asia. Japan's attacking midfielder Shunsuke Nakamura is one of the leading Asian stars playing in Europe.

Shunsuke Nakamura

⚽ Luis Chilavert, goalkeeper for Paraguay, rushed out of his goal and scored for his team in a goal against Argentina in 1998. The final score was 1–1.

⚽ The first person to score from a penalty in a World Cup final was Johan Neeskens for Holland in 1974.

⚽ In the 1994 World Cup finals, Russia failed to qualify for the later stages even though it scored more goals in the first stage of the competition than any other team.

⚽ The referee for the 1930 World Cup final wore a shirt, tie, jacket, and knickerbockers!

John Terry lifting the FA Cup for Chelsea after the 2009 final

⚽ After Brazil beat Italy 4–1 in the 1970 World Cup Final, reporters pursued Pelé into the locker rooms and interviewed him while he took a shower!

⚽ Uruguay, with a population of just three million, is the smallest nation to have won the World Cup.

⚽ The first international soccer game played by a side with 12 players was in 1952, between France and Northern Ireland. One of the French players was injured and substituted, but after treatment he continued playing, and no one noticed until half-time.

⚽ Two pairs of brothers, John and Mel Charles and Len and Ivor Allchurch, played in the Welsh team that beat Northern Ireland 3–2 in 1955. John Charles scored a hat trick.

QUESTIONS AND ANSWERS

Q How many women play soccer in the US?

A Soccer is the most popular women's sport in the US, with around eight million players. USA Women won the first World Cup in 1991 and won it again in 1999. The team has claimed Olympic gold three times—in 1996, 2004, and 2008.

Q Why was the first World Cup held in Uruguay?

A Uruguay, host nation of the first World Cup in 1930, offered to pay travel expenses for all the teams.

Q Were old soccer balls heavier than those used today?

A People make the mistake of thinking that old soccer balls were heavier than those used today. They were virtually the same weight, but today's soccer balls have a special coating that stops the leather from absorbing moisture. Before this development soccer balls could absorb water freely and on wet days the ball could double in weight, often making it as heavy as 2 lb (1 kg).

Kristine Lilly of USA Women

Leather soccer ball

Q When were floodlights first used?

A The first recorded use of floodlights was at Bramall Lane, Sheffield, England, in 1878. The lamps were placed on wooden gantries and were powered by dynamos.

Q When were women banned from playing on the grounds of FA clubs?

A On December 26, 1920, more than 53,000 spectators packed into Everton's Goodison Park to watch Dick Kerr Ladies play St. Helens Ladies. The FA, worried that the women's game was socially unacceptable, banned women from playing on FA club grounds in 1921. The ban was not lifted until 1970!

Q Which country was the first to be knocked out of a World Cup in a penalty shootout?

A Penalty shootouts were introduced into the World Cup Finals in 1982 and in the semifinals West Germany knocked out France.

Q Who plays soccer in the Olympic Games?

A The national women's soccer teams compete in the Olympics, but for men it is the national Under-23 teams that take part.

Q Who was England's first black professional soccer player?

A Arthur Wharton, originally from the Gold Coast (now Ghana), played for Preston North End as an amateur in the 1880s. He then went on to play as a professional for Rotherham Town, Sheffield United, and Stockport County. He was also a gifted sprinter and could run 100 yards (91 m) in 10 seconds.

Q Why have there been three different FA Cup trophies?

A The first trophy was stolen while on display in a Birmingham sports store window, after Aston Villa's 1895 victory, so a second trophy, a replica of the first, was made. When Manchester United won the FA Cup in 1909, it made a copy of this second trophy for one of its directors. As a result, the FA withdrew this trophy and made the third and current FA Cup trophy. Manufactured in 1911, it bears no resemblance to the original 1872 trophy.

Q What does the phrase "back to square one" have to do with soccer?

A When the UK's BBC first broadcast soccer live on the radio in 1927, the *Radio Times* printed a diagram of the field, divided into numbered squares. When the ball was passed back to the goalkeeper, the commentators would say, "Back to square one."

BBC radio microphone

Q When was the first official women's soccer game?

A Netty Honeyball, secretary of the British Ladies Football Club, organized the first women's soccer game in 1895.

Record breakers

- Brazil is the only country to have played in the final stages of every World Cup.

- The oldest soccer club in the world is Sheffield FC. Formed in 1857, the club has always played nonleague soccer.

- Lev Yashin (Russia) is the only goalkeeper who has been chosen as European Footballer of the Year.

- In 1999, Manchester United made history by becoming the first team to win the Triple of the Premier League, the FA Cup, and the European Champions League.

- Real Madrid has won the European Champions League nine times, more than any other team.

- In 1957, Stanley Matthews became the oldest player to play for England when he won his 84th international cap at the age of 42. He continued playing league soccer until he was 50 years old.

Stanley Matthews collector's card

Who's who?

SOCCER IS A GAME OF SPEED and skill, and there are many outstanding players. With international competitions like the FIFA World Cup, extensive media coverage, and a transfer system that allows players to sign for clubs in other countries, players from all parts of the world can become household names. Referees can also build up a considerable reputation around the world. These pages contain some of the past and present players who are among the world's best.

Italian referee Pierluigi Collina

GOALKEEPERS

- SEPP MAIER, WEST GERMANY, B.2.28.44
The pinnacle of Maier's distinguished career was in 1974, when he won the European Cup with Bayern Munich, followed by the World Cup with West Germany. He played with Bayern Munich for a total of 19 years.

- PETER SHILTON, ENGLAND, B.9.18.49
Renowned for his fitness and perfectionism, Shilton made his senior England debut when he was only 20 years old. Over the next 21 years he played for his country 125 times.

- PETER SCHMEICHEL, DENMARK, B.11.18.63
Schmeichel moved to Manchester United in 1991, where he won five league titles and two FA Cups. In his trademark "star" save, Schmeichel runs out, spreads his arms and legs wide, and jumps toward the striker.

- DINO ZOFF, ITALY, B.2.28.42
Tall and determined, Zoff was almost impossible to beat. He appeared 112 times for Italy between 1968 and 1983 and captained Italy when it won the World Cup in 1982. With club side Juventus, he won six Italian League titles and the UEFA Cup.

- JÚLIO CÉSAR SOARES, BRAZIL, B.9.3.79
A natural born leader, Soares controls the defense for Italian side Internazionale, regularly making world-class saves and winning international awards as a result.

Júlio César Soares

DEFENDERS

Paolo Maldini

- PAOLO MALDINI, ITALY, B.6.26.68
An attacking fullback and one of the best defenders in the world, Maldini captained AC Milan and Italy, appearing for Italy more than 120 times.

- MARCEL DESAILLY, FRANCE, B.9.7.68
Born in Accra, Ghana, Desailly moved to France when he was a child. In 1993 and 1994, he won the Champions Cup twice, first with Marseille, and then with AC Milan. Desailly played a vital role for the French national team when it won the 1998 World Cup and the European Championship in 2000.

- PAUL BREITNER, WEST GERMANY, B.9.5.51
An adventurous, skilled left back at Bayern Munich, Breitner moved forward to midfield on transferring to Real Madrid. He was relaxed and seemingly nerveless in big games.

- ROBERTO CARLOS DA SILVA, BRAZIL, B.4.10.73
A player of great skill, with a reputation for taking ferocious free kicks, Roberto Carlos entered the Brazilian national team after the 1994 World Cup. A runner-up in 1998, he won the World Cup in 2002. He joined Real Madrid in 1996, winning the Spanish league in his first season and the UEFA Champions League Final in his second.

- FERNANDO RUIZ HIERRO, SPAIN, B.3.23.68
A gifted central defender, Hierro's surefooted tackling helped Real Madrid to win the UEFA Champions League Finals in both 1998 and 2002.

- FRANCO BARESI, ITALY, B.5.8.60
The best sweeper in the world for much of the 1980s and 1990s, Baresi would bring the ball forward and join in attacks. He retired in 1997, having played more than 600 times for club team AC Milan during his 20-year career.

Bobby Moore

- BOBBY MOORE, ENGLAND, B.4.12.41—D.2.24.93
A gifted defender and an excellent captain, Bobby Moore led England to victory in the 1966 World Cup. He played for England 108 times, only missing 10 matches between 1962 and 1972.

- OSCAR RUGGERI, ARGENTINA, B.1.26.62
Ruggeri was the heart of the Argentine defense in the 1980s, and a World Cup winner in Mexico in 1986. He captained his national side and won a total of 89 caps.

MIDFIELDERS

- **LUIS FILIPE MADEIRA CAEIRO FIGO, PORTUGAL, B.11.4.72**
Figo was a European champion at under-16 level in 1989, and a World Youth Cup winner in 1991. He won the Portuguese Cup with Sporting Clube in 1995, and moved to Barcelona, where he captained the team to the Spanish league title in 1998, before moving on to play for Real Madrid.

- **PAUL GASCOIGNE, ENGLAND, B.5.27.67**
An extremely gifted player who possessed excellent ball control and passing skills, Gascoigne's career was hampered by injuries. He was an important member of England's 1990 World Cup team.

- **ALAIN GIRESSE, FRANCE, B.9.2.52**
A skillful player with excellent technique, Giresse was at the heart of the French midfield at the World Cup finals in 1982 and for the 1984 European Championships.

- **FRANK RIJKAARD, HOLLAND, B.9.30.62**
Rijkaard made his debut for Holland at the age of 19. A universally admired and versatile player, he played midfield for Milan but central defense for Holland. He moved around Europe, playing for clubs in Holland, Portugal, Spain, and Italy.

- **FRANCK RIBÉRY, FRANCE, B.4.7.83**
The great Zinédine Zidane labeled Franck Ribéry "the jewel of French soccer" and no wonder. His frightening pace and accurate passing have ensured his place in the Bayern Munich and France teams, as well as the accolade of Germany's Footballer of the Year in 2008.

- **VITOR FERREIRA BARBOSA (RIVALDO), BRAZIL, B.4.19.74**
A fast, attacking midfielder, Rivaldo has skillful ball control and excellent passing skills. A great creator of goals, he can shoot with either foot, and is often successful with unorthodox overhead shots. He was a key player in the Brazilian national squad in the 1990s and was awarded FIFA World Player of the Year in 1999.

Franck Ribéry

- **SÓCRATES, BRAZIL, B.2.19.54**
A player with tremendous balance and poise, Sócrates made excellent passes, but also scored terrific goals. He studied to be a doctor before becoming a soccer player, and returned to medicine once his playing days were over.

- **ZINÉDINE ZIDANE, FRANCE, B.6.23.72**
An outstandingly skillful player, Zidane was voted Young Player of the Year in 1992. He scored two goals in his national debut for France. He was FIFA's World Player of the Year both in 1998 and in 2000. A creative and inspirational player who was composed and confident on the field, he scored two of his country's three goals against Brazil in the 1998 World Cup Final in Paris, becoming a French national hero.

Sócrates

FORWARDS

- **ROBERTO BAGGIO, ITALY, B.2.18.67**
A gifted goalscorer, Baggio helped Juventus win the UEFA Cup in 1993 and the league title in 1995. He was FIFA's World Player of the Year and European Footballer of the Year for 1993.

- **GEORGE BEST, NORTHERN IRELAND, B.5.22.46—D.11.25.2005**
An amazingly gifted player, Best had brilliant ball skills and excellent balance. He was European Footballer of the Year in 1968. Many feel that he could have played at the highest level for longer had the success of his club side, Manchester United, continued.

- **KENNY DALGLISH, SCOTLAND, B.3.4.51**
Dalglish was probably Scotland's greatest-ever player. His ball-control skills were excellent, and he could slice through a defense with his bold, accurate passes.

- **THIERRY HENRY, FRANCE, B.8.17.77**
A striker possessing terrific ball control, incredible pace, and clinical finishing, Henry was top goalscorer for France when it won the World Cup in 1998.

- **RAUL GONZALEZ BLANCO, SPAIN, B.6.27.77**
An extremely gifted player with a knack for being in the right place at the right time, Raul scores stunning goals, both with his head and his feet.

- **RONALDO LUIS NAZARIO, BRAZIL, B.9.22.76**
Ronaldo scored his first goal for Brazil when he was only 16 years of age. An exciting, inspirational striker, his speed and skill enable him to break through almost any defense. Ronaldo was FIFA's World Player of the Year in both 1996 and 1997.

- **KARL-HEINZ RUMMENIGGE, WEST GERMANY, B.9.25.55**
European Footballer of the Year in 1980 and 1981, Rummenigge was a formidable forward capable of cutting through a team's defense. Between 1976 and 1986 he appeared 95 times for West Germany, scoring 45 goals.

George Best

Wayne Rooney

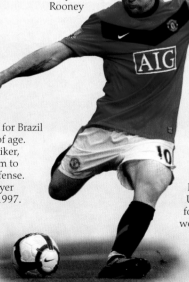

- **WAYNE ROONEY, ENGLAND, B.10.24.85**
Rooney burst onto the Premier League stage at the age of 16 and starred for England in the 2004 European Championships two years later. Manchester United's powerful forward has already won the Premier League three times and the Champions League in 2008.

- **CHRISTIAN VIERI, ITALY, B.7.12.73**
A fast, decisive striker, Vieri ended his first season with Madrid in 1998 as the Spanish league's top scorer, with 24 goals. He scored five more for Italy in the 1998 World Cup finals.

World Cup wonders

Since the first World Cup in 1930, the competition has grown in size and stature, with a global audience of 715 million people watching the 2006 Final and 32 teams set to participate in 2010. The World Cup's colorful history is packed with super scorers, memorable moments, and amazing anecdotes.

WINNERS

Only seven countries have ever lifted the World Cup trophy:

Country	Years
BRAZIL	1958, 1962, 1970, 1994, 2002
ITALY	1934, 1938, 1982, 2006
GERMANY	1954, 1974, 1990
ARGENTINA	1978, 1986
URUGUAY	1930, 1950
ENGLAND	1966
FRANCE	1998

Italy lifts the World Cup in 2006

HIGH SCORES

The highest score in the World Cup Finals was in 1982, when Hungary beat El Salvador 10–1.

The highest score in a World Cup qualifier came on April 11, 2001, when Australia thrashed American Samoa 31-0.

It's a knockout
During the World Cup finals of 1958, a Brazilian player named Vava scored against the Soviet Union. His teammates mobbed him with such enthusiasm that he was left unconscious on the field and needed medical treatment!

GREATEST GOALSCORERS

RONALDO (BRAZIL)
15 goals   1994–2006

GERD MULLER (WEST GERMANY)
14 goals   1966–1974

JUST FONTAINE (FRANCE)
13 goals   1958

PELÉ (BRAZIL)
12 goals   1958–1970

JÜRGEN KLINSMANN (GERMANY)
11 goals   1990–1998

SANDOR KOCSIS (HUNGARY)
11 goals   1954

Brazil's Ronaldo

Hat-trick heaven
When Brazil and Poland played in the 1938 World Cup, Brazil's Leônidas da Silva scored a hat trick followed by a fourth goal. In response, Poland's Ernst Willimowski hammered in three, then another to level the score. Brazil's Romeo finally got the game-winner in overtime.

YOUNGEST PLAYER
Northern Ireland's Norman Whiteside was 17 years old when he played in the 1982 World Cup.

OLDEST PLAYER
Cameroon's Roger Milla was 42 years old when he played in the 1994 World Cup.

FASTEST GOALS
AFTER KICK-OFF

HAKAN SUKUR	(TURKEY) vs. SOUTH KOREA 2002	11 seconds
VACLAV MASEK	(CZECHOSLOVAKIA) vs. MEXICO 1962	15 seconds
ERNST LEHNER	(GERMANY) vs. AUSTRIA 1934	25 seconds
BRYAN ROBSON	(ENGLAND) vs. FRANCE 1982	28 seconds
BERNARD LACOMBE	(FRANCE) vs. ITALY 1978	31 seconds

GETTING THE BOOT
India withdrew from the World Cup in 1950 in protest at the rule stating that all players must wear boots.

TROPHY TRIVIA

NEW TROPHY

⚽ The existing World Cup trophy was first awarded in 1974. The name and year of every World Cup winner is added to the bottom of the trophy. In 2038, a new trophy will be used because there won't be enough space left for new names on the current one.

⚽ The trophy is made of 18-carat gold! It stands 14 in (36 cm) high and weighs 13 lb (6 kg).

OLD TROPHY

⚽ The original trophy was called the Jules Rimet Trophy in honor of the FIFA president from 1921 to 1954. The Frenchman was a key figure in bringing soccer to the world stage and setting up the first Finals in 1930.

⚽ The trophy was stolen twice. The first theft was in England in 1966, but a dog named Pickles later discovered it. The trophy was then stolen again in Rio de Janeiro in 1983 and has never been found. It is believed to have been melted down.

Zakumi, South Africa's 2010 mascot

© 2007 FIFA TM

MASCOT
Zakumi is the official mascot for the 2010 World Cup in South Africa. The leopard with green hair is named after "ZA," the international abbreviation for South Africa, and "kumi," the word for "10" in many African languages. He is yellow and green like the host nation's uniform.

ROYAL REQUEST
At the first World Cup held in Uruguay in 1930, the Romanian team was handpicked by King Carol, who organized time off work for the players!

2010 STADIUMS

⚽ On March 17, 2006, FIFA announced the 10 stadiums set to be used for the 2010 World Cup. Located all over South Africa, these included two stadiums in Johannesburg as well as venues in Durban, Cape Town, Pretoria, Port Elizabeth, Bloemfontein, Pietersburg, Nelspruit, and Rustenburg.

⚽ The capacity of the South Africa stadiums ranges from 40,000 spectators up to 95,000.

⚽ Built in 1987, Soccer City Stadium in Johannesburg is the country's first international soccer stadium and remains the largest venue for the 2010 World Cup.

⚽ With a capacity of 70,000, the Moses Mabhida Stadium in Durban is a brand-new building for 2010, on the site of the old Kings Park Soccer Stadium, which was torn down in 2006.

Royal Bafokeng Stadium, South Africa

BLANCO BOUNCE

The 1998 World Cup Finals in France saw the introduction of a new soccer trick, courtesy of the Mexican player Cuauhtémoc Blanco. He broke through the defense by wedging the ball between his feet and jumping.

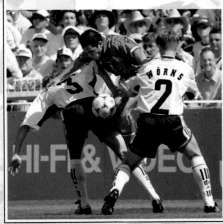

Soccer playing nations

T HE BEAUTIFUL GAME is played all over the world on streets, fields, parks, and beaches. In each country, the most gifted players join their national teams to compete in high-profile tournaments. Whether the side has a history of success or no titles to date, fans dream of winning soccer's top tournament, the World Cup.

ENGLAND

Believed to be the founder of modern soccer, England and the nation's fans have a long-standing love of the game, with the stand-out moment coming in 1966, when the team won the World Cup.

Football Association founded: 1863
Nicknames: The Three Lions
Top goalscorer: Bobby Charlton 49 (1958–70)
Most appearances: Peter Shilton 125 (1970–90)
Trophies: FIFA World Cup—1966

ARGENTINA

This South American country has a vibrant soccer history, with memorable moments, fanatical fans, and a packed trophy case.

Argentinian Football Association founded: 1891
Nicknames: Albicelestes (White and Sky Blues), Los Gauchos (The Cowboys)
Top goalscorer: Gabriel Batistuta 56 (1991–2002)
Most appearances: Javier Zanetti 135 (1994–present)
Trophies: FIFA World Cup—1978, 1986
Copa America—1921, 1925, 1927, 1929, 1937, 1941, 1945, 1946, 1947, 1955, 1957, 1959 (round-robin league tournaments), 1991 (round-robin, then final round of four teams in a mini league), 1993
Olympic gold medal—2004, 2008

FRANCE

With a penchant for attacking soccer, France is the epitome of entertainment. Although the team did not win an international trophy until 1984, it has made up for lost time by winning the World Cup and European Championship in recent years.

French Federation of Football founded: 1919
Nicknames: Les Bleus (The Blues)
Top goalscorer: Thierry Henry 48 (1997–present)
Most appearances: Lilian Thuram 142 (1994–2008)
Trophies: FIFA World Cup—1998
UEFA European Championship—1984, 2000
Olympic gold medal—1984
FIFA Confederations Cup—2001, 2003

AUSTRALIA

Although Australia dominates in many major sports, soccer is not one of them. Following years of success in Oceania, the country joined the more competitive Asian Football Confederation in 2006.

Australian Soccer Association founded: 1961
Nicknames: Socceroos
Top goalscorer: Damian Mori 29 (1992–2002)
Most appearances: Alex Tobin 87 (1988–98)
Trophies: Oceania Football Confederation (OFC) Nations Cup—1980, 1996, 2000, 2004

GERMANY

Thanks to great teamwork and skill on the ball, Germany has an unrivaled record for consistency, reaching 12 major competitive finals and winning six tournaments.

German Football Association founded: 1900
Nicknames: Die Nationalelf (The National Eleven)
Top goalscorer: Gerd Muller 68 (1966–74)
Most appearances: Lothar Matthaus 150 (1980–2000)
Trophies: FIFA World Cup—1954, 1974, 1990
UEFA European Championship—1972, 1980, 1996
Olympic gold medal—1976

BRAZIL

The most successful soccer-playing nation in history, Brazil has won the World Cup a record-breaking five times with a long line of legendary players.

Brazilian Football Confederation founded: 1914
Nicknames: A Selecao (The Selected), Canarinho (Little Canary)
Top goalscorer: Pelé 77 (1957–71)
Most appearances: Cafu 142 (1990–2006)
Trophies: FIFA World Cup—1958 1962, 1970, 1994, 2002
Copa America—1919, 1922, 1949, 1989, 1997, 1999, 2004, 2007

ITALY

The world's second most successful soccer-playing nation after Brazil, Italy has four World Cups to its name. Solid defensive play and fast counterattacks are integral to the team's winning ways.

Italian Football Federation founded: 1898
Nicknames: Azzurri (Blues)
Top goalscorer: Luigi Riva 35 (1965–74)
Most appearances: Paolo Maldini 126 (1988–2002)
Trophies: FIFA World Cup—1934, 1938, 1982, 2006
UEFA European Championship—1968
Olympic gold medal—1936

DENMARK

Although the nation has produced many quality players, the team has yet to enjoy continued success. The highlight to date was Euro 1992, when Denmark caused a shock by beating West Germany in the final.

Football Association founded: 1889
Top goalscorer: Poul "Tist" Nielsen 52 (1910–25)
Most appearances: Peter Schmeichel 129 (1987–2001)
Trophies: UEFA European Championship—1992
Confederations Cup—1995

IVORY COAST

An exciting new prospect in international soccer, the Ivory Coast reached the World Cup finals in 2006 and many of the nation's homegrown talents now play for great European clubs in their domestic leagues.

Ivory Coast Football Federation founded: 1960
Nicknames: Les Elephants (The Elephants)
Top goalscorer: Didier Drogba 38 (2002–present)
Most appearances: Cyrille Domoraud 51 (1995–2006)
Trophies: African Cup of Nations—1992

JAPAN

Soccer is now the second most popular sport in Japan, following two triumphs in the Asian Cup and a successful co-hosting and encouraging performance in the 2002 World Cup.

Japan Football Association founded: 1921
Nicknames: Nihon Daihyo (Japanese Representatives), Blues
Top goalscorer: Kunishige Kamamoto 74 (1964–77)
Most appearances: Masami Ihara 122 (1988–99)
Trophies: AFC Asian Cup—1992, 2000, 2004

REPUBLIC OF KOREA

Hopes are high for the Republic of Korea after co-hosting the World Cup finals in 2002. The nation drew international recognition by unexpectedly reaching the semifinals, knocking out favorites Italy and Spain along the way.

Korea Football Association founded: 1928
Nicknames: Taeguk Warriors, Tigers, Red Devils
Top goalscorer: Cha Bum-Kun 55 (1972–86)
Most appearances: Hong Myung-Bo 135 (1990–2002)
Trophies: AFC Asian Cup—1956, 1960

MEXICO

A dominant force in the CONCACAF, boasting Latin brilliance on the ball, Mexico is rapidly establishing itself as a serious contender in international competitions.

Mexican Football Federation founded: 1927
Top goalscorer: Jared Borgetti 46 (1997–present)
Most appearances: Claudio Suarez (1992–2006)
Trophies: CONCACAF Championship and Gold Cup—1965, 1971, 1977 (round-robin team tournaments), 1977 (top World Cup qualifying team awarded trophy), 1993, 1996, 1998, 2003
Confederations Cup—1999

NETHERLANDS

In the 1970s, the Dutch created "Total Soccer," a system in which every player could play in every position on the field. This fluid formation coupled with legendary players has resulted in impressive play but, surprisingly, just one title.

Royal Netherlands Football Association founded: 1889
Nicknames: Clockwork Orange, The Orangemen, Flying Dutchmen
Top goalscorer: Patrick Kluivert 40 (1994–2004)
Most appearances: Edwin van der Sar 130 (1995–present)
Trophies: UEFA European Championship—1988

PORTUGAL

Under the influential management of Felipe Scolari, Portugal achieved success by reaching the European Championship final in 2004 and the World Cup semifinals in 2006, but is still yet to win a title.

Portuguese Football Federation founded: 1914
Top goalscorer: Pauleta 47 (1997–2006)
Most appearances: Luis Figo 127 (1991–2006)
Trophies: None

RUSSIA

Although the nation has not won a major title for 50 years, exciting new talents and effective teamwork combine to give Russia a strong basis for future success in international competitions.

Russian Football Union founded: 1912
Top goalscorer: Vladimir Beschastnykh 26 (1992–2003)
Most appearances: Viktor Onopko 109 (1992–2004)
Trophies: (competing as the USSR)
UEFA European Championship—1960
(competing as Russia) None

SOUTH AFRICA

Following 30 years of exile by FIFA for refusing to field a mixed-race team, South Africa is now going from strength to strength, culminating in 2010, when it becomes the first African nation to host the World Cup.

South African Football Association founded: 1991
Nicknames: Bafana Bafana (The Boys)
Top goalscorer: Benni McCarthy 31 (1997–present)
Most appearances: Shaun Bartlett 74 (1995–2005)
Trophies: African Nations Cup—1996

SPAIN

Despite celebrated players and great spirit, the Spanish team has been prone to underachieving in the past. However, it is now realizing its potential, thanks to success in the 2008 European Championship and the development of rising stars such as Cesc Fabregas.

Royal Spanish Football Federation founded: 1913
Nicknames: La Furia Roja (The Red Fury), La Seleccion (The Selection)
Top goalscorer: Raúl 44 (1996–2006)
Most appearances: Andoni Zubizaretta 126 (1985–98)
Trophies: UEFA European Championship—1964, 2008
Olympic gold medal—1992

URUGUAY

Famous for being the first nation to lift the World Cup in 1930, Uruguay repeated this success 20 years later. These early achievements have been followed by triumphs over the years in the Copa America, but it is yet to recapture its former glory in the World Cup.

Uruguay Football Federation founded: 1900
Nicknames: La Celeste (The Sky Blue)
Top goalscorer: Hector Scarone 31 (unknown–1930)
Most appearances: Rodolfo Rodriguez 78 (unknown–1994)
Trophies: FIFA World Cup—1930, 1950
Copa America—1916, 1917, 1920, 1923, 1924, 1926, 1935, 1942, 1956, 1959, 1967, 1959, 1967 (round-robin league tournaments), 1983, 1987, 1995
Olympic Games—1924, 1928

USA

The soccer-playing reputation of the nation that came somewhat late to the game has improved greatly since it hosted the World Cup in 1994. Qualifying for every World Cup since has shown the critics that the US is here to stay as a serious competitor.

United States Soccer Federation founded: 1913
Nicknames: The Stars and Stripes, The Red, White, and Blue
Top goalscorer: Landon Donovan 41 (2000–present)
Most appearances: Cobi Jones 164 (1992–2004)
Trophies: CONCACAF Gold Cup—1991, 2002, 2005, 2007

Find out more

THERE ARE MANY WAYS of getting more involved in the world of soccer. An important start is to find a club you want to support, and follow its performance. If you like to play yourself, you can join a team and take part in a local league. By visiting museums such as the National Soccer Hall of Fame, for example, you will find out about managers, coaches, and scouts as well as players, and will build up a picture of the world of soccer. The more you learn, the more you will enjoy the soccer fever surrounding the big competitions, such as the World Cup Finals.

REMEMBER THE MATCH
Programs are full of information about the teams that are playing and are also a great keepsake of an exciting event.

Bob Bishop was the Manchester United scout who discovered George Best, Sammy McIlroy, and many others in the 1960s and 1970s

---

USEFUL WEBSITES

- For news and information on the World Cup, visit: www.fifa.com
- Interested in playing soccer yourself? Check out the online home of the AYSO for tips on joining a team in your area: www.ayso.org
- To get the latest news on American Major League Soccer, go straight to the MLS website: www.mlsnet.com
- To follow the US Men's and Women's national teams, go to: www.ussoccer.com
- This BBC site features international soccer news, plus videos to help you with your skills: news.bbc.co.uk/sport2/hi/football/

SUPPORT YOUR TEAM
Decide which team you want to support and start following its results. If you can, go to some games and start your own collection of programs. Watching the games and reading the programs you will soon become an expert on your team's players and management. You will learn about soccer rules and will have your own ideas on tactics, and how the team should be run. If you get a chance to go to an international game, you will meet soccer fans from other parts of the world.

SOCCER SCOUTS
All big clubs have scouts who travel around looking for new talent, whether it be established players that the club can "buy," or gifted youth players. Outstanding young players will be asked to participate in a trial, and if successful, may be invited to join the club's training academy. Here they will receive a general education as well as intensive soccer training. If all goes well, they will work up through the youth and reserve teams to play on the club's first-string team.

Italian fans cheer for their team

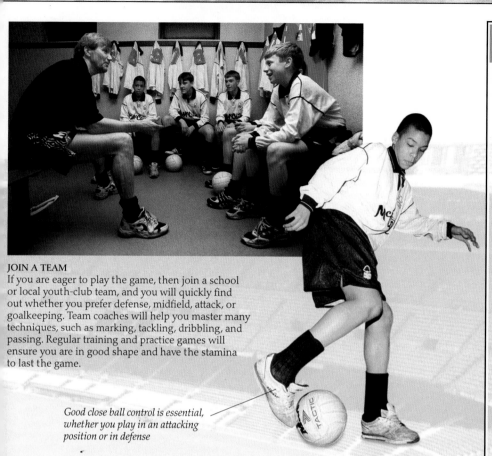

JOIN A TEAM

If you are eager to play the game, then join a school or local youth-club team, and you will quickly find out whether you prefer defense, midfield, attack, or goalkeeping. Team coaches will help you master many techniques, such as marking, tackling, dribbling, and passing. Regular training and practice games will ensure you are in good shape and have the stamina to last the game.

Good close ball control is essential, whether you play in an attacking position or in defense

THE 2010 FIFA WORLD CUP

In the summer of 2010, the FIFA World Cup Finals will take place in South Africa. There have been 19 World Cups played so far, but this is the first time that an African nation has hosted the competition. South Africa qualifies automatically as the host nation and another 31 teams from around the world will join it, based on the results of qualifying games. Stadiums in Johannesburg, Cape Town, and Durban are among the official venues.

Places to visit

In all FIFA competitions, a Fair Play Trophy is awarded to the team with the best behavior

FIFA fair play logo, introduced in 1993

Glossary

AFRICAN NATIONS CUP First won in 1957. African national teams compete for the trophy every two years.

AGENT The person who acts on behalf of a player in the arrangement of a transfer or a new contract.

ASSISTANT REFEREES Formerly known as linesmen, one covers each side of the field. They signal offside, throw-ins, fouls, and substitutions.

BOOK The referee books players when they have committed an offense. He shows players a yellow card and writes their names in his black book. Players are sent off if they receive two yellow cards in one game.

CAP Originally a hat awarded to those playing an international game. Players count their international appearances in caps.

COACH Runs the training program, working closely with the manager.

COPA AMERICA CUP First won in 1910. North and South American national teams compete for the trophy every two years.

CORNER KICK Awarded when one of the defending team has put the ball out of play over the goal line.

CROSS A pass made from either wing to a forward at the center of the field.

DEAD-BALL KICK A kick from non-open play, such as a free kick or a corner kick.

A referee's uniform

DERBY A derby "game" is a game between two local rival teams.

DIRECT FREE KICK Awarded if a player kicks, trips, pushes, spits, or holds an opponent, or tackles the player rather than the ball. The person taking the free kick can shoot directly at the goal.

DIRECTORS The people who serve on a board to help run a club. Some put a lot of personal money into the club.

DRIBBLING Running with the ball while keeping it under close control.

EUROPEAN CUP
First won in 1956, it is now known as the Champions League. The top clubs from the league of each European country compete for the trophy every year.

FA CUP First won in 1872. English league and non-league teams compete annually for the trophy.

Using your chest to control the ball

FIFA (FÉDÉRATION INTERNATIONALE DE FOOTBALL ASSOCIATION) Formed in 1904. The world governing body of soccer, FIFA sets international rules, arbitrates between countries, and runs the World Cup.

FOOTBALL ASSOCIATION Formed in 1863. The governing body of English soccer arbitrates between clubs and disciplines players.

FORMATION The arrangement of the players on the field. The coach or manager chooses the formation, and may change it during a game in response to the strengths or weaknesses of the opposition.

GIANT KILLER A team that beats a side believed to be of a much higher quality, and from a higher division.

GLOVES Worn by goalkeepers to protect their hands and to help them grip the ball.

GOAL KICK Awarded when the ball goes out of play over the goal line if it was last touched by the attacking team.

GROUNDKEEPERS The people who look after the stadium, the stands, and the soccer field.

HANDBALL It is an offense to touch the ball with your hands or arms during play.

HEADING A defensive header sends the ball upward, clearing it as far away as possible. An attacking header sends the ball downward, hopefully into the goal.

INDIRECT FREE KICK Awarded for dangerous play or for blocking an opponent. The player cannot score directly.

The white ball was introduced in 1951

KICKOFF The kicking of the ball from the center point of the field to start the game.

LAWS The 17 Laws of the Game approved by FIFA.

MANAGER The person who picks the team, plans tactics, motivates the players, and decides what to do in training.

MARKING Staying close to an opponent to prevent him from passing, shooting, or receiving the ball.

MASCOT A person, animal, or doll that is considered to bring good luck to a team. Mascots are also part of the increasing commercialization of soccer.

HIGHGROVE

70

OFFSIDE When an attacking player receives a ball, two defenders including the goalkeeper have to be between the attacking player and the goal. Players are only penalized for being offside if they interfere with play or gain some advantage by being in that position.

ONE-TWO An attacking player passes the ball to an advanced teammate and runs on into a space. The ball is immediately returned, bypassing the defending player.

PENALTY AREA A box that stretches 18 yd (16.5 m) in front of and to either side of the goal.

PENALTY KICK A shot at the goal from the penalty spot. Awarded against a team that commits an offense in its own penalty area.

PENALTY SPOT The spot 14 yd (13 m) in front of the goal. The ball is placed here to take a penalty.

PHYSICAL THERAPIST The person who helps players recover from injuries, and who checks players to make sure that they are well enough for a game.

FIELD The field of play. In the early days the boundaries of the field were marked by a series of flags. The FA introduced the field markings we know today in 1902.

PROGRAM Provides information for the fans about the players of their team and of the opposition, as well as a message from the manager.

RATTLE Supporters took rattles into games until the 1960s, when they started to sing or chant instead. Today, rattles are forbidden.

RED CARD The referee holds up a red card to show that a player has to leave the field. Serious foul play or two bookable offenses results in a red card.

REFEREE The person who has authority for that game to enforce the Laws of the Game.

SCARF Each team has a scarf in its own colors. Fans often wear the scarf or their team's uniform when they go to games.

SCOUT A person employed by a club to look for talented new players.

SET PIECE Moves practiced by a team to take advantage of a dead-ball situation.

SHIN PADS Pads worn inside socks to protect the lower legs.

SHOOTING A kick toward the goal.

PLAYER'S CIGARETTES

KICKING TO SWERVE THE BALL

A soccer card

STANDS The areas where the supporters sit or stand around the field.

STRIP The shirt, shorts, and socks a team wears. Most clubs have at least two strips, a home and an away uniform. A team uses its away uniform when there is a conflict of colors.

STUDS (OR CLEATS) Small rounded projections screwed into the sole of a soccer shoe. The referee or assistant referee checks all studs before play starts. Players use longer studs on a wet, muddy field.

SUPERSTITIONS Many players are deeply superstitious. For example, they may insist on wearing the same shirt number throughout their career. England player Paul Ince would only put his shirt on for a game when running out of the tunnel.

TACKLING Stopping an opponent who has the ball and removing the ball with your feet.

TACTICS Planned actions or movements to gain an advantage over your opponents.

TERRACES Steps where people stood to watch a game before the advent of all-seater stadiums.

THROW-IN A way of restarting play when the ball goes over the touchline. Awarded to the opponent of the player who last touched the ball.

UEFA EUROPA LEAGUE Originally known as the Inter City Fairs Cup. First won in 1958. Changed its name to UEFA Cup and was renamed UEFA Europa League in 2009/10. Some of the best teams from each European country's national league compete for the trophy every year.

World Cup medal

WARM-UP A routine of exercises to warm up all the muscles before the start of a game.

WHISTLE Used by the referee at the beginning and end of a game and to stop play when there is a foul.

WINGER A striker who plays particularly on one side of the field or the other.

WOMEN'S WORLD CUP First won in 1991. National women's teams compete for the trophy every four years.

WORLD CUP First won in 1930. National men's teams compete for the trophy every four years.

YELLOW CARD The referee holds up a yellow card to book a player.

The US Women's soccer team, 1998

Index

Acknowledgments

Dorling Kindersley would like to thank Hugh Hornby, Rob Pratten, Lynsey Jones, & Mark Bushell at The National Football Museum for their help and patience; Stewart J. Wild for proofreading; Hilary Bird for the index; David Ekholm-JAlbum, Sunita Gahir, David Goldblatt, Susan St. Louis, Lisa Stock, & Bulent Yusuf for the clipart; Neville Graham, Sue Nicholson, & Susan St. Louis for the wallchart.
The publishers would also like to thank the following for their kind permission to reproduce their photographs:
a=above; c=center; b=below; l=left; r=right; t=top; f=far; n=near

Action Images: Jason Cairnduff 57c; Jean Marie Hervio / Flash Press 16cl, 31crb; Toby Melville / Reuters 27cra; Carl Racine 63crb; Bruno Domingos / Reuters 56r; Sporting Images 23c; Sporting Pictures 22c. Action Plus: Glyn Kirk 56c; Neil Tingle 10fbr, 60-61 (background), 68b. Colorsport: 11tr, 21br, 32clb, 39tr, 44-45, 57tr, 68tl; Olympia 35cr, 35tr; Jerome Provost 39bc. Corbis: Matthew Ashton / AMA / Corbis Sports 65cr; Matthew Ashton / Corbis Sports 60cb; S Carmona 44clb; Paul Haigh / EPA 60cr; Stephane Reix / Corbis Sports 66-67 (background); Brett Whitesell / Corbis Sports 61tl. Dorling Kindersley: Football Museum, Preston / 1974 FIFA TM 48r; Football Museum, Preston / Adidas 18br; Football Museum, Preston / FIFA 46fbr (1998), 49fcr; Football Museum, Preston / Sondico 31ftr; Football Museum, Preston / Umbro 28br; Football Museum, Preston 1, 2bc, 2c, 2cl, 2cla (rubber tube), 2clb, 2fbl, 2fcl, 2ftl (brass pump), 2ftr, 2tc, 2tl (gauged pump), 3c, 3ftl, 3ftr, 4bc, 4bl, 4br (pin), 4cla, 4crb, 4fbl, 4fbr (ball), 4fbr (boot), 4tl, 4tr, 5br, 5fbr, 5ftl, 5ftr (brazil), 5ftr (italy), 5tl, 5tr (dutch), 5tr (hungary), 6b, 6c, 6fcra, 6tr, 7bc, 7cb, 7crb, 7l, 7tr, 8c, 8ca, 8fbr, 8ftr, 8l, 8tr, 9br, 9cr, 9crb, 9fclb, 9l, 9tr, 10cb, 10clb, 10fclb, 10tl, 10-11, 12br, 12cb (whistle), 12fclb, 12tl, 12tr, 13br, 13cr, 13ftr (bangladesh), 13ftr (columbia), 13ftr (italy), 13ftr (new zealand), 13ftr (usa), 13tr (australia), 13tr (iceland), 13tr (portugal), 13tr (usa), 14br, 14ca, 14t, 14-15, 15bl, 15cl, 15clb, 15cb (side view), 15cr, 16tl, 17br, 18bl, 18cb, 18cr, 18tl, 18tr, 19bl, 19tl, 20bl, 20cr, 20tl, 20tr, 21bl, 21cra, 21crb, 21tr, 22cla, 22tl, 22tr, 22-23, 24bc, 24cl, 24crb, 24ftl, 24tr, 25bl, 25cb, 25crb, 25ftl (brass), 25ftl (gauged pump), 25ftr, 25tl (pump), 25tl (rubber), 25tr, 26br, 26cl, 26cr, 26tl, 26tr, 27bc (hammer), 27bc (studs), 27br (nails), 27br (studs), 27c, 27cla, 27fbr (key), 27fbr (studs), 27fbr (wrench), 27tl, 28bl, 28crb, 28tl, 29bl, 29cr, 29tl, 29tr, 30br, 30c, 30cl, 30crb, 30tl, 30tr, 31bc, 31bl, 31clb, 31tl, 31tr, 31br, 36bc, 36cb, 36cl, 36clb, 36cra, 36fbr, 36fcl, 36fcrb, 36ftl, 36ftr, 36tr, 36tr (spoon), 37bl, 37br, 37c, 37clb, 37cr, 37fbl, 37fcrb, 37tr, 38bl, 38br, 38tl, 38-39, 39cr, 39tl, 40b, 40ca, 40cb, 40cl, 40crb, 40ftl, 40ftr, 40tr, 41ca, 41cl, 41clb, 41tr, 42cr, 42tl, 42tr, 43br, 43cra, 43fcr, 43ftr, 44ftr, 44tl, 44tr, 45cl, 45t, 46bc (1986), 46bl (1978), 46bl (1982), 46br (1990), 46br (1994), 46c (1954), 46c (1958), 46cl (1938), 46cl (1950), 46clb (1930), 46clb (1934), 46cr (1962), 46fcr (1966), 46fcrb (1970), 46fcrb (1974), 46tl, 46tr, 47br, 47tr, 48bl, 48tl, 49cr, 49ftl, 49tl, 49tr, 50cl, 50tl, 50tr, 51tl, 52br, 52c, 52fbl, 52fcl, 52ftl, 52-53, 53bc, 53bl, 53cla, 53cr, 56tr, 57crb, 61br, 70tc, 71cla; Mark Leech 43bl; The Science Museum, London 61tr. FIFA: 69br; 2007 FIFA TM 65tc. Getty Images: 62cr, 63tr; AFP Photo / Pierre-Philippe Marcou 58tl; AFP Photo / Roberto Schmidt 50c; AFP Photo DDP / Thomas Lohnes 58b; Allsport 34-35; Allsport / Hulton Archive 48bl; Allsport / Scott R Indermaur 43tl; Allsport / Vincent Laforet 50br; Lars Baron / Bongarts 63cla; Shaun Botterill 62-63 (background); Shaun Botterill / Getty Images Sport 64-65; Clive Brunskill 14bl; David Cannon / Allsport 33c, 51r; David Cannon / Getty Images Sport 23tl, 64cl; Central Press / Hulton Archive 32cla, 33cr; Jonathan Daniel 71br; Tony Duffy / Allsport 32br; Mike Hewitt / FIFA 2r; Mike Hewitt / Getty Images Sport 16r; Keystone / Hulton Archive 33bl, 33tl, 34tl; Ross Kinnaird 58c; David Leah 51c; John Macdougall / AFP / 2005 FIFA TM 69clb; Clive Mason 17tl; Damien Meyer / AFP 13l, 17bl, 62bl; Paolo Nucci / WireImage 49bl; Doug Pensinger / Getty Images Sport 17c; Popperfoto.com 68cl; Gary M. Prior 62tr; Mark Ralston / AFP 27tr; Bob Thomas 21l; Michael Urban / AFP 36bl; Alexandra Winkler / Reuters 59tr. Bryan Horsnell: 42c, 42cl, 42fcl. Press

Association Images: AP Photo / Lewis Whyld 44cla; Matthew Ashton / Empics Ltd 68-69 (background); Matthew Ashton / Empics Sport 16tr; Jon Buckle / Empics Ltd 70-71 (background); Adam Davy / Empics Sport 62c; Empics Ltd 32tr; Alastair Grant / Associated Press 71tr; Laurence Griffiths / Empics Ltd 69ca, 69tl; Tony Marshall / Empics Sport 28tr; Don Morley / Empics Sport 34tr; PA Archive 34bc; Peter Robinson 63bl; Peter Robinson / Empics 47l; Peter Robinson / Empics Sport 34tc, 57fcrb; Neal Simpson / Empics Sport 38cl; Michael Steele / Empics Sport 41br, 41fclb; Topham Picturepoint 35tl; Witters 32ftr.

Wallchart: Colorsport: cl (biggs), cla (villa). Corbis: Franck Seguin / TempSport cb (stadium). Dorling Kindersley: Football Museum, Preston / Adidas fbl (shin pads); Football Museum, Preston cr (cards), fcr (ref); ftl (kinnaird), tl (chinese writing), tr (toy); Puma fclb (boot side), fclb (boots sole). Getty Images: David Leah / Allsport / FIFA fcrb (world cup); Claudio Villa c (messi).

All other images © Dorling Kindersley
For further information see:
www.dkimages.com